WHITE WOMAN WITCHDOCTOR

WHITE WOMAN WITCHDOCTOR

TALES OF THE AFRICAN LIFE OF RAE GRAHAM

AS TOLD TO

TAFFY GOULD MCCALLUM

Fielden Books / Miami, Florida

FIELDEN BOOKS
145 SOUTHEAST 25TH ROAD
MIAMI, FLORIDA 33129
305 / 856.5645

AMAGI BOOKS
P. O. BOX 92385
NORWOOD 2117
SOUTH AFRICA
011 / 442.8898

Distributed by
COUNCIL OAK BOOKS
1350 EAST FIFTEENTH STREET
TULSA, OKLAHOMA 74120
1-800 / 247.8850
IN OKLAHOMA 918 / 587.6454

DESIGNED BY CAROL HARALSON.

ISBN NUMBER 0-9633721-8-1

LIBRARY OF CONGRESS CARD CATALOG NUMBER 92-72451

Printed in the United States of America.

In memory of my father, Emil J. Gould,
who delighted in and supported my work,
and in honor of my mother, Estelle Gould,
who has always joined him in that delight
and support.

CONTENTS

ACKNOWLEDGMENTS

I would like to express my appreciation to a number of people for their assistance in the production of this book: to Iris Saltzman of the International Para-Psychology School in Miami, Florida, for her insights into psychic readings; to Jack Morten of Greencorp USA, Inc., for audio tapes; to Margot and Arthur Amoils of Johannesburg, South Africa, for their generous and always gracious hospitality; to Cecil Graham for his help in the taping of interviews and for checking facts and details and corroborating or correcting Rae's memory; to Col. A.T. House and Milton Sadoff for their computer expertise and indulgence; to Kate Bandos, Robert Clifton-Bligh, Perley Noll, Audrey Renault, and Milton Sadoff for their patient and thorough reading of the manuscript and for their gentle but beneficial suggestions.

TGMcC

BOTSWANA

KALAHARI DESERT

Mochudi●

Venda

Sibasa●

TRANSVAAL

Johannesburg
●

ORANGE FREE
STATE

NATAL

CAPE PROVINCE

Durban
●

R E P U B L I C   O F
S O U T H   A F R I C A

Cape Town
●

MAP OF
THE REPUBLIC OF
SOUTH AFRICA

INTRODUCTION

I first met Johannesburg City Councillor Rae Graham while gathering material for a book on the women of South Africa's twenty-one diverse societies. I had been told that she had lived in Venda for many years and could give me some insight into the women of that land before I ventured there.

As I arrived at her home—on a hill above Johannesburg, once the site of the home of an early mining engineer — I was immediately struck by her extensive collection of Venda art and artifacts. By the time I left, two hours later, I had been enthralled by the stories of her adventures among the Venda people. Only later, when I returned to South Africa to spend some one hundred hours interviewing her for this book, did I learn that those adventures (and misadventures) extended to Botswana, to the Kalahari Desert among the Bushmen, and to a great many other venues, as one of the very few white witchdoctors in the country.

Rae Graham has been called "the blackest white in South Africa." She is also known as "the bridge," for her work explaining blacks to whites and whites to blacks in her adopted country. More than once has the irony been noted that it took a British nurse from "the wrong side of the railway line" in Bristol, England, to cross the gulf after crossing an ocean and to make some of the first early inroads into inter-racial understanding. Among blacks, Rae is known as Mashudu ("Lucky One") and, as an honorary member of the Venda tribe, she had bestowed upon her by the Venda Chief the title Makhadzi ("my sister by another mother").

It may be said that all white African lives are unconventional—certainly by most Western standards. To some, the life means adventure, mystery and romance; to others it is primitive, full of hardship. Of those who "came out" from England, many returned, unable to deal with the harsh realities of "an uncivilised world." Of those who stayed, some created a "little England" of elegant homes, tea parties, clubs and private schools, cricket and horseracing. Rae Graham, who came out from England as a new bride in 1948, might have led the elegant life, but she did not. Fate dealt her a different hand.

The stories which follow are but a fraction of those I heard. Some made me laugh heartily; others brought tears to my eyes. Not a few left me speechless. I have chosen to recount them here as closely as possible in Rae's own words. To tell her story in the third person would, I feel, detract from their immediacy and intimacy and rob them of their spontaneity.

TGMcC

A celebration in the Shangaan tribal area. Women and men sit separately.

ABOVE: *A metal bracelet maker in Sibasa under the large old tree opposite the Graham trading station.* BELOW: *Rae Graham (Mashudu) and Venda women playing the drums at a chief's ceremony.* FACING PAGE, TOP: *The Sibasa Trading Store.* FACING PAGE, BOTTOM: *The marketplace in Sibasa opposite Rae and Cecil Graham's home.*

TOP: *Venda girls dancing whilst at Domba.*
BOTTOM LEFT: *Domba drummers.* BOTTOM
RIGHT: *At the boys' inititation school in Venda.*

Top: *Venda girls at the girls' initiation school.* Bottom: *A dancer at the boys' inititation school in Venda.*

ABOVE: The Domba ceremony in Venda. RIGHT: A full set of drums around the fire, to heat, tighten, and tune up the skins. Sibasa, Venda.

CLOCKWISE FROM UPPER LEFT: *1. Nyamugoza with a murumba drum which has a special pocket for snuff. 2. Nyamugoza (the master of Domba) with a ngoma drum. 3. A mbila tshipai player. 4. A dende player.*

TOP: *Venda pots and dishes.* BOTTOM: *Ralushai, a herbalist, sitting opposite the Graham Trading Store in Sibasa.*

MUSINGS

I knew I was going to have to do this thing, that is, to become a witchdoctor.

I always say to people, "Don't think you've got to be in the bush to be in Africa?" They always assume that to get to the real Africa you've got to get in a truck and go out somewhere rural. It's not true: The real Africa is all around us.

Every time I was in Checkers or the OK [grocery or department store], I was looking for what the whites call a witchdoctor. I knew what to look for because they wear a telltale necklace. Even if they're in formal suits and shirts you can see the bump of the shape of that particular necklace. If it were jewellery it would be worn outside; if it was hidden, it was obviously the professional trade necklace. I've got mine. You're supposed to wear it forever, once you graduate, but they know that I cannot, as I have two lives, and if I'm wearing low-neckline garments in Council, I can't be wearing a witchdoctor's necklace.

One day when I was down in the shops I saw this man and I went up to him and touched him and I greeted him in his language and said, "Please, I know what you are; will you come home with me?" "No, no," he said. "I'm shopping for my madam." And I said, "Well, phone her and tell her you've broken down or broken your leg or something, but please, please come home with me. I want to talk to you about your profession." And he did! I suppose it was so unusual that a white would ask him this sort of question — and in his own language — that he was bowled over.

So I brought him to my home in my car. When he saw my front door, which is pure Venda — carved wood and anthropologically accurate — he was already halfway in my hands. When he entered the house and saw all my Venda artifacts — not what one normally would expect to find in the home of an ordinary white woman — he related immediately.

Then I sat down on the floor, on the skins, and said, "Join me. You may find this quite extraordinary, but I want to train to become an *nyanga* (a witchdoctor; pronounced as in-yahng´-a). When I lived in Venda, they said, 'you can't just learn it like learning the piano; you have to join and belong,' but I couldn't do it then because I had young children and didn't have the kind of time to set aside. But I've got it now."

He said to me, "I can't say 'yes' or 'no'; I can't make that kind of decision. But I will talk it over with the other Vendas." So I took him back to Checkers and he went home, and that was the end of that.

A long time went by, but I had sown the seed. Eventually I was sent for by a man who worked over in another suburb. This is a fascinating situation: He's an incredible gardener because he's an herbalist, and he grows *muti* round the roses. His employers are very fond of him, but they don't understand why he has so many visitors as soon as his workday is over. They don't understand why there's a flood of people coming there until midnight. When I first went there, they thought I was trying to steal their gardener! Of course there were so many people because at night he was doing his work as a witchdoctor.

In any case, on that one day many years ago, some men came to my house and told me they would have to test me out locally before they made the big decision on whether or not I could train to be a witchdoctor. They took me to where this man worked and we picked him up and brought him back to my home. He sat down and threw the bones and told me, "There isn't a definite 'no' here, but there isn't a definite 'yes,' and I cannot take that kind of responsibility. But things will happen." Now that's typically black. You don't say when, where, or how. But I felt really quite chuffed [elated] because it was looking friendly. They were sizing me up.

Then I became quite ill. I got pneumonia and it was really very bad. My lungs were full of fluid and I went to bed. My doctor, who is very tolerant of my black life — in fact, he's been quite supportive — came to see me and asked, "What do your witchdoctor friends say?" and he laughed. I told him I hadn't been to see them yet.

As soon as the blacks heard that I'd been very ill, all the doors were wide open. When you are called to this profession in the black world you are always very ill first. Always. The fact that I got pneumonia was, therefore, very propitious.

One day, they came to fetch me. Two of them — an *nyanga* and a *mongoma* (another kind of witchdoctor). They said to Cecil (whom they always call "Cicil"), "We have to take her away, to find out this thing." And Cecil said, "That's fine; where are you going? And for how long?" "We're going away for five days," they told him. "Can I phone her?" "No. There will be no roads, no telephones, no form of communication. But we will bring her back." So Cecil said, "Fine. Cheerio, dear." He didn't mind. (But, I always tell people, he doubled my life insurance!) And off I went.

It was the most incredible five days of my life. But that's getting ahead of the story. How did it all begin . . . ?

EARLY LIFE IN ENGLAND

I always go back to the day I was married — August 23, 1948, in Bristol, England. An Anglican church because my husband was Anglican. I was Methodist — a lay preacher, actually. I used to go out to the pubs and tell everybody to stop drinking! But when I fell in love with Cecil and we were planning our wedding, I said, "Well, you've got nobody here in England who will be at the wedding, and at least I have some family, so we'll get married in your church."

It was a cold, rainy day, and a typically English wedding. We were miserable, but we had a ball at the reception. We had with us all the people we knew we would never see again. They were there to say goodbye. But what struck me very forcibly — and to this day I can feel it — was that, as I stood there and the minister asked Cecil, "Do you take this woman to be your lawfully wedded wife?" I thought to myself, Boy, that's the word: TAKE. Where am I going? We'd discussed South Africa, and he'd tried to explain to me about Bechuanaland (now Botswana), where he grew up — where his parents originally had been traders before they moved to trade in Venda, another black country to the north — and I knew I was going to Bechuanaland, and that it was a hot and dusty country with eight Tswana tribes in it. He'd explained it to me; he tried to tell me what my way of life was going to be. But suddenly, as I got married, the very moment the minister asked that question, I was scared. I thought to myself, I don't really know what I've taken on. All I knew was that I trusted the man I was marrying.

My life up until then had not been very happy. Growing up during the war was not a happy experience. I was born with three sisters in a very humble home on the wrong side of the railway line, and in

England that counts. There were no laws or prejudice, as there is in South Africa, against race or colour, but in England, boy, it surely counted whether you were above or below the tracks. We were below the tracks. My mother married when she was seventeen to a man whom she adored in a flashing moment, but it was a very unsuccessful marriage, a very unhappy marriage. My father was an uneducated man who was strong and angry and arrogant, and he had four daughters, which didn't please him.

My mother died when I was nearly eight years old. My younger sister and I were sent to live in an orphanage and I looked after my little Melody. She is fifteen months younger than I, but we were desperately close because we had to rely on each other. (Our two other sisters were ten years older. I don't really remember ever living with them. We must have, but I don't really remember that period.) Some time after that we were taken out to go live with a housekeeper woman who was dreadful, so my childhood wasn't very happy. Much later, when my father married again, we did have a happy time for a couple of years, with our stepmother.

I was a bright child and won a full scholarship to a private school — Redmaid, a top school like Roedean in Johannesburg. You had to have long hair with red bows. It was very exclusive. But I won! I took a First, and my photograph was in the local paper. I remember it very well. I was twelve years old. I remember the passion. I wanted very much to go. The people from Redmaid came to the house and interviewed us, and they said to my father, "This won't cost you anything. She gets her books and uniform and she lives in. Will you allow your daughter to go?" And he said, "No. I had no education and she needs no education. And anyway, she needs to go out and work, soon." They tried hard to persuade him to let me go, but he wouldn't. I cried and cried and begged him, but to no avail. I never understood it. Up to this day I still don't understand it, but that's the way it was. I had always had a passion for learning, for wanting to know everything, but I was stopped.

When I was thirteen and a half I went out to work, because in those days you could apply not to go to school if you had to work to help your family. It was not at all as it is now, because back then there were many disadvantaged people who couldn't go to school. I went to work in a packing factory, packing boxes and earning seven shillings and sixpence [$1.50] a week. I remember that very well, and treating my sister on a Saturday to a thruppence bioscope [movie] with a penny orange drink — that's what I did every single Saturday. Then the war progressed to a stage where, when I was sixteen, the government dropped the age for nursing. (The war had been on all this time. I grew up during the war. Every single night there were bombs and I never went to a bedroom to sleep for years. We slept in cupboards under the stairs, fully dressed.)

Before the war you had to be twenty-one with matric [high school diploma], for nursing. Then it got down to age eighteen without matric, then down to sixteen without any qualifications at all, and that opened up a door for me. That's what the war did for me. Dreadful thing to say, but the war gave me my chance in life. I said goodbye to my father, my stepmother, and my sisters — who were not really at home much — and I was on my way to become a nurse. You could live in, you got a uniform, you got food, and you got certain other things, like free cinema tickets and free bus rides, and that was my chance.

I failed many exams for the first two years, because although I'm a natural nurse, it had been years since I'd done any studying. The Matrons used to ask me, "Why is it that you nurse so well but fail the exams? How come you never make it yet you're so good in the wards?" "I don't know," I said, "but the books scare me." I plodded along, and I had many friends who helped me, and eventually I graduated with a diploma as a State Registered Nurse.

During the war I became one of the youngest Night Sisters — age nineteen and running a whole hospital. I was the most senior person at night. I remember a plane coming down one night: I got a phone call that there was a German pilot who was alive in the district, injured, and that he would most likely try to make it to the house of the doctor or to the hospital. I got all my nurses together and got them all to get brooms and brushes and spades for protection. In every ward there was a trembling nurse with her weapons. The front doorbell rang and I got them all together and opened the door. There, on the door step, was a woman about to have a baby! Poor woman, she looked up and saw all these nurses with brooms and spades and nearly had her baby there and then! The German pilot did pitch up at the doctor's house, in the village. He was about twenty years old, like us, and he was scared rotten. He had a broken leg, but of course that meant he was safe for the rest of the war. He's living in Germany now, and I'd love to meet him.

Eventually, I went right through to become one of the youngest Matrons in the hospital. Then I had a wonderful time when the American army came into the war.

We were in a forest in the middle of England — because of the bombing — in a prefab military section of the hospital. My patients were quite mixed — free Poles, POWs of different nationalities, the whole lot. When the Americans came, bringing all their modern equipment, it was a new era, and we were all very much more alive. After a while I met an American soldier named Harry Shearer, from Rochester, New York. He had a twin sister, Harriet, with whom I corresponded. I knew Harry for two years and we became engaged. I loved him dearly. Came the day when he came to see me to say goodbye. He had his helmet on, and I said, "Harry, take your helmet off," and he refused. Then I knew, because the day the paratroopers were dropped in occupied Europe, they shaved off the soldiers' hair. If ever you saw a man with no hair, you knew he was on the next drop. And so I knew that this was goodbye. We didn't say much, and then he was gone. The next day he was killed in the air, still in his parachute; he didn't even touch ground. What a waste. As with many thousands of others, all that beautiful youth. I didn't get over that for years. I was so young, yet I felt my life was empty. We had been very close. The fact that I now have two daughters who are Americans — married to Americans — and three American grandchildren, is an indication to me that the bond to the USA was meant to be. I was meant to have an American connection — very special. My husband, Cecil, knows all about Harry and the deep impression he had on me. Harry was a gentle, kind soul; the war was anathema to him.

The Americans who came over in the army, the medical section, came into my life in my hospital. They worked with us. They were surgeons with the best equipment I had ever seen, because, you see, we had been in the war so long that we had run out of everything. This is terribly important, when I come to my *nyanga* [witchdoctor] life, and I always relate it in my lectures.

At this time I heard about Mr May and Mr Baker, who had just produced the first "M and B" (sulfa) drugs. They gave us this new material, asking for the patients to be fully monitored — blood pressure, pulse, temperature, etc. — and given a certain diet. No eggs or milk. It was very much an investigatory exercise. I have said to my daughter, who is a Nursing Sister in San Jose, California, "So easy it is today; everything is ordered with exact dosages, and you know the results to expect." But I was there at the birth of this brand new substance. It was exciting and stimulating for all of us. Later, in my black life, I started using natural substances and testing elements; it made sense to me because I had done it in my white life. Also, it is important to realise that prior to the Americans' arrival I had had to make do and mend a great deal. Not just me; all the nurses in all the hospitals were in the same position. Every night in the hospital we used to wash all the bandages. All the corridors were hanging with drying bandages, because I didn't dare throw them away. Even the rubber gloves were used again and again. The night nurses spent their free time mending them, cutting up the really old ones to use for patches, and many times even the patches were patched yet again, in an effort to provide something for the surgeons to wear. Sometimes, during operations, the surgeon would peel off his glove and throw it down exclaiming, "I can't work in that, Sister!" and I would reply, "That or nothing." That's how low we were in supplies.

We also used many "home remedies." I used to take grey clay, into which we would place various substances, spread the clay onto white felt material and place it on top of a boiling fish kettle, to heat it up. This poultice would then be placed onto patients' infections, and it helped. To break a high temperature there is a simple remedy that often is successful: Place the patient between wool blankets and have beside him a bowl of boiling hot water and a bowl of iced water. Dip towels into both and alternately bathe the patient — hot, cold, hot, cold until the patient starts to sweat and his temperature is lowered. It takes time, and like many things we did then, it was hard work. Indeed, nursing was very hard work then, very physical. There were not that many drugs to do the job. Nursing today is more technical; for us it was very physical, and patients stayed in bed for weeks, not days. With our greater patient contact, we also had greater bonding.

Very often we were without electricity, and my fish kettle boiled on gas to sterilise instruments. We continued to make poultices on the kettle lids. Tea leaves are excellent for burns. After all, they contain tannic acid, which is what you find in the prepared creams from the chemist [pharmacist]. A compress of cold tea takes away pain immediately and commences healing. I don't know how I acquired these tips; I only remember that we were often thrown on our own resources.

I was not in a city at this time, but in a country hospital in a village near Marlborough. I got to know all that area quite well. Marlborough is a special Heritage Village, and we were in the Savernake Forest, nearby. It was beautiful there. One day, two American surgeons came to see me and said, "Hi there, what's your name?" I said, "Sister Panes, sir; what's yours?" "George," said one of them. "Oh, no," I said. "It's not like that here, sir. No first names." They thought that was hilarious, but anyhow I got to love them dearly. George opened up a small suitcase and said, "Sister, could you get these things sterilised and we'll get going." I stood there breathless, with my hands behind my back, and said, "I have never seen such perfect instruments. Everything we have has been broken and mended and recreated again." The war had been on a for long time. When America sent us stuff by ship, it often ended up on the bottom of the ocean. So that's how it was.

By this time I was doing a lot of brain theatre [surgery] work. I loved it. I had a gut feel for it and I enjoyed the work. I sterilised all this wonderful new equipment and called all the nurses to come and have a look, and we were like a lot of hens clucking round the trolley [cart]. I then started working with these men regularly. They came into our lives as they were giving of themselves to England before they would ultimately go overseas and off to the front. They were fantastic and a joy to work with.

I also had American soldier patients. Two of them I will never forget: Mr Potter and Mr Moore. At that time there was a range of face creams in England called Potter and Moore (nothing to do with these two soldiers). It was a well-known make of British make-up and it was elegant to use it. Now into my life came these two gentlemen with the same names. Mr Potter was white and Mr Moore was coal black — and both in the same ward. Mr Moore was the first black man I had ever met. The very first one; that's why I remember him. I decided one day to make the patients laugh, because life was pretty grim for them and a lot of them were going to die. We did a service to the patients called a "back round" where you roll the patient onto his side, wash his bottom with warm water and soap, and then rub him with methylated spirits — rubbing well to get the circulation going and to prevent bedsores, ending up the exercise with talcum powder. The patient feels much better, afterwards, for the movement in sore areas. I always used white talcum powder and it looked like an iced chocolate cake, when I did Mr Moore's tail end, so on this occasion I sprinkled him with cocoa, much to everyone's amusement. He could hear everyone laughing and asked, "What are you doing there, Sister?" And I said, "I wish you could see your bum; you are now chocolate coated!"

And so I started with good American material and American influence, which was super. This American contact in my life has been often and always good.

I then moved to a large hospital in Oxford. Actually, I worked in three different hospitals in Oxford. I was a Sister in the Radcliffe Infirmary, where I was doing a lot of brain theatre work, and I kept notes on how things progressed. Just as aeroplane pilots painted their planes with how many enemy they had shot down, I too kept records, but of a different sort. Unfortunately, brain surgery was not as advanced, then, as it is today, and very few patients recovered. My records were of how few died on the operating table. We worked quickly, when the op was done, to fix up the patients and get them back to the ward. We lived with a lot of death and had to learn to cope with it in our own way. Success was to complete the op well and then get the patient quickly down the passage to the ward. We were all very young because the older people were overseas in the war itself.

We had to learn to cope, psychologically, with death in our own age group. To understand what I am, and why I am what I am, is to understand the circumstances in which I grew up. Relying on one's own inner self and strength was a daily need. I often cried myself to sleep when someone I had nursed and grown very close to died. I was only sixteen years old when I started nursing, and I had to assist a woman in delivering her baby when I was seventeen, with no midwifery training. It was me or no one. I said to the woman, "Tell me what to do," and she asked, "Is this your first baby?" When I said, "Yes," she replied, "Thank God it's not my first!" I was the only one there; there was no one else around, so we got on with it. It was an unusual way to grow up, but I have no regrets. I wouldn't have grown up any other way: I found and developed all my own inner resources. We got used to death, and we got used to patients being missing from their beds, knowing they had died.

Some time later I was a Ward Sister again and I had a large ward full of soldiers straight from the front, all of them seriously injured, full of shrapnel, etc. In the basement of the hospital, Professor Florey and Professor Fleming were producing a brand new substance called penicillin — a growing fungus, not the synthetic kind we all use today. A natural growth from nature, not an artificial, manmade product. The ward of broken, shredded men was quite a sight — most of them in plaster casts with limbs that smelt of rotting flesh. They all had [intravenous] drips up — saline and glucose, plasma, etc. — and when penicillin was given to us to use, there were no rules because no one knew exactly what would happen with it. It was introduced into the drips and we monitored the reaction.

I can remember one young man with mangled hands just lying there. He wanted a cigarette to be placed within his lips. He used to shout out aggressively, "Give me a cigarette!" and we would give him one. When you are completely helpless and frightened and having difficulty coping, it is natural to get aggressive. Professor Florey's wife, who was very deaf and had an ear trumpet that she held to one ear, came near to this boy and leaned over, and he quickly kissed her. It was his way of expressing thanks. She loved all these boys and they loved her. They would always try to get her to come close.

The two professors did not have time to come round the wards, due to the pressure of work. But they were men of incredible ability. Mrs Florey was a brilliant doctor in her own right, and it was only her the boys saw. All those boys would cajole her to their side. Most of them couldn't move much, but they would grab her and kiss her. It was deeply moving. I have wonderful memories. To use that natural substance —

penicillin — from the Lord made sense to me. Since then it has gone so much further, but it was exciting to be in on its beginnings.

CECIL

met Cecil in unusual circumstances. I had a weekend leave and went by train to London, where I had a great time seeing shows, etc. (During the war one didn't travel much, so I had grown up not knowing my own country. The bombing was too bad, so I had never been to London. I have only really got to know England as a tourist, when we go over on visits. Funny, really. But with my thirst for knowledge, I now know it quite well, just as I have got to know South Africa. So much due to my burning search for knowledge, because I didn't get it formally. Probably the best gift my father could have given me — the denial of schooling — for now I have learnt so much more.)

My weekend leave in London I stayed in uniform, as there were many free theatres for nurses, but also because I didn't have any money for clothes. When I started nursing the salary was15 pounds [$60] per year, but we received somewhere to live, food, and uniforms, so it was fine. I remember, though, hating those monthly queues at Matron's office for one free tube of toothpaste and one packet of sanitary towels, and the loss of pride because we couldn't afford *not* to take those things. As a Sister I earned £3 [$12] a month, which was a lot of money at that time.

Having spotted Cecil in one of the compartments of the train (all trains were divided into compartments, then), I placed my little suitcase inside that one and deliberately fell over it at his feet! He picked me up, of course, and then it was easy to have conversation. He bought me tea, and we decided to meet again. Having got him to pick me up, I decided I would marry him! It took two years to reach that point, but I knew immediately that this was the man I wanted to marry.

He started to tell me about himself, that he was South African and was in the volunteer army, and that his Division had been allocated to the American army in Italy. He fought there from the tip right up through the top, living in dugouts and suffering the ice and snow. He was about twenty-four when we met; I was twenty-one. I remember there was a long time of over a year from Harry's death before I would even consider a date. My family were so concerned, my two brothers-in-law would take me out dancing and I would say, "Forget it; stop trying. My heart is dead." And then, much later, I met Cecil and I felt all was well. There had been no one in between. I remember that I had no real attachment when I turned twenty-one, because on my birthday it was a nothing day with no remembrances.

I did have one real birthday in my youth — only one — when I was nine. My mother had died and I was living with her mother, who was going blind. I was placed with her for some time to be her eyes. Everywhere we went, her hand was placed on my shoulder, and I would verbally warn her of approaching steps, street crossings, etc. I can still feel that hand's presence and our closeness. I've been back there, to her church, and have given a talk to that community, and they remembered us being together. She was very good to me and for my birthday gave me a garden party with paper lanterns hanging in the trees, and a cake. So much did it mean to me that I remember having a new yellow and white dress — something that hadn't happened often. When I gave the talk in the church, some years ago, some of the old ladies had tears in their eyes, and afterwards, when I talked to them, they told me they remembered my mother and said I was just like her. That was a wonderful feeling, to experience their regard for a mother I can't really remember.

Cecil had been at the University of the Witwatersrand (Wits) for less than a year when he joined up as a volunteer in the South African army, and after a brief period of basic training was sent to join the 6th South African Armoured Division at the end of the desert war. The division then went over to Italy to form part of the US 5th Army, under General Mark Clark, and Cecil remained with that Division until the end of the Italian Campaign in May, 1945. He had wanted to go to university in England, so his mother pulled a few strings through the then Vice Chancellor of Wits, Professor Raikes, and he was seconded to the British 8th Army just long enough to be flown from Italy to England in a Lancaster bomber converted into a troop carrier. He was demobilised there, received the British standard civilian demobilisation kit, and went up to Oxford in October, 1945, to start his university education. He read [majored in] English and ultimately gained his M.A. degree. Oxford, and I presume other English universities, gave priority to foreign students and to people whose academic careers had been interrupted by the war, so not many English school leavers [high school graduates] were accepted. Oxford was unusual, then, for having very few school graduates on campus. Rather, it was mainly men, men who had suffered and were suffering symptoms and difficulties in living a rehabilitation [normal] life again. Men without an arm or a leg, men in wheelchairs and on crutches. Oxford will never have a period like that again. We all looked fairly young, but in life's experiences we were not young. There were New Zealanders, Australians, South Africans. There were Jews from concentration camps and men who had been shut off from help, in underground movements. I knew them all. It was different. We have been back as visitors to see beautiful Oxford, where we had first got to know each other, and it was so strange. I said, "Look, Cecil, the place is full of *kids*." For us it was men.

This was one of the first difficulties I had to come to grips with in my marriage: my husband with an Oxon M.A. in English and me with my Standard Five [seventh grade] education. You can't get a much bigger gap than that. We were both fully aware of this problem, so he arranged for me to go to night school whilst I was still a nurse, and I attended classes in literature and music appreciation. I had also learnt typing and shorthand as an asset. When Cecil discovered this, he asked if I would come to lectures on my free times and take notes for him, so I did. At Oxford they don't have a register for open lectures, and his friends never let on that I was actually not a student. Having taken down all the notes of those really difficult lectures — difficult for me, that is — I then had to transcribe them into English for Cecil — a very good learning exercise for me. When he finaly graduated, I was at the ceremony, and as he was capped, I felt very much a part of it. Indeed, his friends told me that part of that degree was mine!

The lecturer for my literature classes was blind and I watched, fascinated, as he read the Braille books to us. He inspired in me a love of good English which I have had ever since. He introduced us to the

Greats. What a new life was opening up for me! At the end of each lesson, I would wait and ask if I could walk him home, and he would smile and say, "You don't have to, you know. I can see very well with my stick." "I know that," I said, "but I want to talk more to you. Tell me more." "Why," he asked, "do you never stop asking questions?" "I don't know," I replied, "but there is so much to know, and I'm starved."

In the meantime, my friendship with Cecil continued unchanged for two years and I was inwardly heartbroken, because I now really loved him. I went up to London, in answer to an advertisement, had an interview, and after some time with investigations I was accepted for a post in Australia, as a District Nurse in the Outback — with a horse to travel and a large district to cover. This really appealed to me, and I felt a breakaway was essential for my own good. When I was advised that I had been chosen, I was half sad, half happy. I took the train down to Bristol and said goodbye to my sisters, then went back to Oxford to work off my last two weeks. I told Cecil that I had signed a contract, and that was it. He wished me well and the next day gave me a book, *Waltzing Mathilda, All You Need to Know About Becoming a Good Aussie.* I said, "Thank you very much" and — back at the hospital — cried my heart out. It was all terribly final.

Ten days before I was due to go, Cecil phoned and begged to see me. Sitting in a little old English pub, he said he couldn't bear to think he would never see me again and would I marry him? "Yes, please," I said. "It's taken you a long time, but Yes." And then the next day I had to go back to London and say I wouldn't take the Australia job. They were very disappointed, but they understood.

One reason I had been keen to go to Australia was that I was very keen on horses. When I was nursing in my first hospital — I was about eighteen then — we had regularly, in the ward, small young jockeys with fractured shoulder bones. When you're thrown off a horse, you hit the ground with your shoulder. I nursed the jockeys and got very fond of the whole stable. This was good breeding stock, safe from the bombs, in the Savernake Forest area, up on the Downs. The well-known jockey, Gordon Richards, was there and loved all his boys. He often came to visit them in hospital, and I got to know him. He discovered my love of horses and offered me free rides whenever I could get off.

Obviously I jumped at the offer and went riding whenever I could.

My sister, Melody, also was keen on this sport. I remember when the war first started, she was thirteen years old and had to go away from us to the centre of England where all the children were placed. I can see her standing on the station platform with a label attached to her coat, with all those hundreds of young children being sent away. I was fifteen, so I didn't have to go. I could work, and also I belonged to the Homeguards and helped to put out fires every night. Melody, however, had a tough time and because of her unhappiness got a nervous disease, St. Vitus Dance. Fortunately, it came right once her life and circumstances changed. We were all parted for so long that the precious few times we were together were indeed very precious. After I became a nurse I would get leave and go and see her, and she would beg me, "Don't leave me here. Please take me with you," but I couldn't. I had nowhere to take her. Once, I did take her for a short holiday and smuggled her into the hospital, into the nurses' home. I put her in a uniform and she lived with me for a week, eating with all the nurses, who never told on us. During a war, with no money, it was the only way we could be together.

When Gordon Richards offered me the chance to ride, I said, "*Me*, ride a horse?" I couldn't believe that my passion for horses could actually be fulfilled. In England at that time, you were *somebody* if you rode: Ordinary folk didn't even contemplate such a luxury. When I went up there to the stables, I said, "I can't ride one of those." "Don't worry," Gordon said, "we've got some hacks, also." I got up, and I can't tell you how I felt. Like gentry. *Me!* I had seen hunters passing through the countryside in their red coats and top hats. It was history. I became quite a good rider, in time, so when I was offered the job in Australia, with a horse, it all fitted together. But that all fell away. I married Cecil.

When Cecil popped the question, he wrote to his parents and told them he was marrying "a nurse called Rae Panes." His mother got on a plane soon after, as she hadn't seen her son for three years and she wanted to meet me. We met in a London hotel, after which Cecil returned to Oxford and I stayed with her for the whole weekend. I was terribly nervous, as you can imagine. During dinner she had said to me, "Are you aware that you use the cutlery incorrectly?" and I had replied,

"Oh, do I? It's just a knife and fork." "Oh, no, it is *not* just a knife and fork," she answered. "Mrs Graham," I said, "I've just come through a war where it really didn't matter very much. Sometimes you were lucky to get any. That's what it's been like." "Oh, yes," she said, "I realise that you have grown up in different circumstances. Do you know about glasses for drinks?" I said, "No, I don't." "Do you know about wine?" "No, but I have drunk it. Your son treats me to wine, but I didn't know the glass was important." And it went on like that. So I watched everything she did, and I copied her. One day, over a meal, she said to me, "The gap between you and my son is enormous. He has the highest form of education and you have the lowest. Are you aware of the gap?" I said, "Yes, we have had difficulties with it, but I love him dearly and I think I could overcome that problem. But Mrs Graham," I said, "I'll tell you what. I love him so much that if you feel I will become a handicap in his life, then you tell me and I will go away forever." I told her about the job in Australia and that I would take that one or another and just disappear, but that she was the one who knew the circumstances here and in South Africa, and so she must decide. "You know what we both are and you know whether or not I will fit. You tell me." Of course she couldn't tell me to go away. So she went back to South Africa, and Cecil and I got married.

Cecil's family could not afford to come over to our wedding. Mother had come before on a single trip, but they certainly could not come again so soon. Cecil did have a young female cousin who was studying music in London, and she came with another young lady friend. The cousin's name was Emmarentia Scheepers, and she eventually changed her name to Emma Renzi — more Italian sounding when she became a great opera soprano in Italy. For some thirty years she sang all the great roles at La Scala and in all the great world theatres. In those days, at weddings, you sat on the side of the church relating to your affiliation to the bride or groom. Cecil's side of the church was going to be pretty empty — just his cousin and friend — so he invited all his Oxford college's cricket team and other student friends. His best friend from the war, Claes Frost — a Dane who had been in occupied Europe in the underground movement — was his Best Man. Claes then went back and became an officer in the Royal Family Guards, in Denmark.

Emmarentia grew up in the Orange Free State, South Africa, and was young and living on her parents' farm and studying the harp when her teacher discovered her great voice. She left home and came overseas to start her career. I asked her to sing at my wedding but she refused, saying, "Oh, no, I couldn't do that. I'm not good enough yet." Imagine, I nearly had the great Emma Renzi singing at my little wedding!

My grandmother (my mother's mother, with whom I had lived as a child) put my wedding together for me, and an aunt paid for the reception. There was very little money but everyone helped, including my three sisters. It was this grandmother who had taught me about life itself. She was a woman of great dignity. When I lived with her she would call me into the bedroom to lace up her tight corset at the back. Every night, when we went to bed, she would take two boxes out from under the bed — a big double bed where we slept together. In one there were lots of strips of cloth, one inch wide, with which she would roll our hair up in small curls and then knots. We would sleep with all these knots all over our heads — most uncomfortable, but in the morning one had nice curls to brush out. We were very fashionable. In the second box were chocolates — rejects from the chocolate factory. Nothing wrong with them except perhaps the printing on top — the design — wasn't quite right, so they were sold as rejects, much cheaper. Every night we had two each and would lie there, side by side, sucking those delicious, marvelous treats. What joy, and I still remember it very well.

My aunt Alice, Grandmother's sister, lived with us, too. She was a hunchback, very short, with rounded shoulders and a pronounced hump on her back. She never married and always did the housework at Grandma's. Her dresses had little capes attached to the shoulders, in an attempt to cover up her deformity.

Once I married Cecil, we toured England and said goodbye to all our dear friends and my family, then went down to Southampton, where we boarded a ship for South Africa. It was October, 1948.

As we set sail for South Africa — there was no one there to see us off — I remember looking at the land receding and thinking to myself, I shan't mind if I never see that land again. My life there had given me so little. I was twenty-three years old, and I desperately wanted to start afresh. I was married on the 23rd August, I was 23 years old, and we said the 23rd Psalm. Three 23s.

We were lucky that Cecil's family had a relative who was a member of Parliament and managed to get us on a ship, when thousands of other people were trying to do the same. It was the old "Windsor Castle" one of the original mail boats between England and South Africa.

This old ship hadn't been fully recommissioned back into service, so it was a bit tatty, and we were out to sea only a few days when most of us got mouth infections. We had to queue up with the ship's doctor to have our mouths painted with gentian violet which, let me tell you, stays on. We all talked with purple mouths. Later on there was a fancy dress party. As Cecil and I had no money for costumes, we had to make something. The ship had stopped at Madeira, where I had purchased some beautiful baskets, so I got the ship's carpenter to make us wooden shoulder yokes, and we dressed up as peasants, carrying baskets on our yokes. To look authentic we got the doctor to paint our faces, necks, and hands with yellow medicine that stained well. We looked really good at the party and won a prize, but the next day the yellow wouldn't come off, so we were purple inside and yellow outside, and that's how we arrived in Durban to meet all my new husband's assembled family!

When we set sail we had only a few Pounds to spend, but we wanted to take part in everything. I said to Cecil, "Don't worry, we'll *make* money." How? Competitions. How many sea miles the ship had done each day — we would win five shillings on that. Then there was a "horse race" competition, where women had to cut a white cotton tape under starter's orders (with a pistol, just like a real horse race.) The difference was that the scissors were curved medical scissors, not straight ones, to make it more difficult to cut in a straight line. But this was a piece of cake for me — I had used curved medical scissors so much in the operating theatre. Not only did I win, but we could place bets on the tote, *knowing* that I probably would win. That night we could celebrate with a martini cocktail because we had made a few Pounds in winnings.

One day there was a contest for the men — a beer drinking competition. There was a large bruiser, an Irish miner, and everyone was betting on him, but I had seen my husband's performance in the Oxford pubs and knew that he could down beer without it ever touching the sides of his mouth. I was queuing at the tote to place all we had £3 [$12] on Cecil, and a gentleman behind me said, "You seem to have great confidence in that slender young man. Do you know something we don't?" "Oh, yes," I said, very proud. "That's my husband, and he can easily outdrink that miner." The Irishman was the favourite because of his swaggering and noisy promises. We kept very quiet. Cecil's rating at the tote [the odds on him] was very high; no one thought he had a chance. Of course he won easily and we had a handsome profit on our £3. Life was very good. The whole two weeks on the boat was such fun and of course was the real holiday that we both needed. At the end of the voyage we had £1 [$4] left.

We arrived in Durban and there on the dock was the family, Father and Mother (Cecil's parents, whom I always addressed as though they were my own) with their big black car and a chauffeur called Nat, the second black man in my life.

They drove us to the Edward Hotel on the seafront, *the* hotel in those days. Very posh. Edwardian in design and named after Prince Edward. I was entranced. It was very British and you "dressed" for every single meal. I had very few clothes — my wedding dress and a few things that Cecil's mother had purchased for me in London. We were taken upstairs to the bridal suite, which had everything — flowers, fruit, and luxury like I had never seen. A porter had helped us upstairs and brought the luggage. Cecil, with a flourish, tipped him with our last and one and only pound. I said, "Cecil, we are now sitting in the bridal suite of the poshest hotel in town and we are absolutely penniless. It might be wise to go and have a visit with your father." Of course there was no worry at all; Father and Mother gave us a wonderful week's holiday, there, whilst we got to know each other. What a time we had! I couldn't believe the shops, with so much in them and no control of coupons, as we had had in England during the war and still had at the time we left

England. Here you could buy anything you wanted. I had grown used to looking in shop windows but never buying anything. I had lived with such constraints that it took a while to fully appreciate this splendid new world. Cecil bought me a whole pineapple for sixpence. All for me. The *whole* pineapple! That was the first thing I wrote home about — that pineapple. Fruit was rationed, in England, and it was mostly for the very young children. My oldest sister had three little daughters and on their special rations they would get bananas. We never got them. So my sister would save one for me, for when I was on leave from the hospital. And here I was with a whole delicious pineapple — and there were plenty for everyone.

I had not seen Mother for about six months — since our first meeting in London. She now took me out shopping, to fit me out with all the things I would need — dresses, hats, shoes, and gloves. Many gloves, in all the colours. Short black for early evening wear, long black for formal wear, three pairs of white (one on, one in the wash, one in the drawer; every lady's requirement). We wore white cotton gloves almost every day. Sometimes it was a nuisance, in a hot climate, to be so dressed, but those were elegant times and ladies were ladies. South Africa was very Victorian in a lot of ways.

I learnt early on about the wearing of gloves. Whenever I went anywhere with Mother in the daytime we wore white cotton gloves. Handbags were made with an envelope portion on the outside, the perfect place to hold gloves when not being worn. One day in Johannesburg, we went out to afternoon tea at the Wanderers Club. Very posh. Nat, the chauffeur, drove us there. I was careful to copy everything Mother did and it went very well. It was elegant and quietly successful. The waiters all were Indian, because the black people were not doing those jobs yet. Whilst tea was taking place I noticed that Mother took off only her right hand glove, not both, so of course I did the same. In the car on the way home I asked her about this and she said, "It is very vulgar to bare your left hand and display your diamonds." As I wasn't exactly loaded down with gems, it pleased me very much to keep my glove on! A great leveller, don't you think?

I do have a beautiful engagement ring — a ruby surrounded by diamonds in a rose design. Cecil of course could not afford such a ring in England, and of course stones like that were not available there. During the war the only rings available were with small cheap diamonds, nothing really nice. Cecil wrote to his mother and she had my ring made in a jeweller's in Johannesburg. Then she mailed it to South Africa House in London. Came the day when we went up to collect it and got engaged on the steps of that grand building. Later, Princess Margaret had an identical ring made for her engagement, but I must stress that mine came first! She had very good taste, not so? Everywhere I went, people would exclaim, "You've got Princess Margaret's ring!" "Oh, no," I would say, "She's got mine!" Cecil did subsequently pay for the ring himself.

It was also vulgar to hear the clink of cup and saucer, so a doily was placed on each saucer. They were hand crocheted. You would also show your good breeding by always taking little sandwiches and canapes first, then perhaps a scone, and last some cake.

Mother also took us out to the gardens in the park, where they served "cream teas" — very formal, in very beautiful surroundings. Many of Cecil's relatives were there to meet me. I was offered a cream scone and took one on my plate but did not immediately eat it. I was so enjoying just looking at it. A troop of monkeys was nearby, in the trees, and quick as a flash one of them rushed down and grabbed my scone and was off! I was close to tears when I saw my treasure disappear, but Mother said, "There, there. It's all right. Have another." And of course there was another and another and another. I wrote home and said, "You won't believe this country; it's full of stuff and full of food. People are eating all the time, and it's so cheap. And you can have *anything!*" This plentifulness was something I had to get used to. Many years later, a black woman friend said to me, "We can always tell who are the white British women in your age group: You never waste any food." I am still like that, today.

The week in Durban was a week I remember with great joy. Some relatives came down from their sheep farm and we sat on the sandy beaches, talking. Other family members were traders in the outlying black areas, and obviously I asked many questions about that life, because I was about to embark on an identical one. Mother and I got on very well. She was fond of me as a person and had come to terms with me as a daughter-in-law, though she remained apprehensive about our marriage relationship.

One morning, Father took us outside the hotel to a rickshaw pulled by a large Zulu, dressed in tribal finery. For a small sum we were pulled along the Promenade — what a ride, what excitement! This was my first encounter with a tribal man, and it made a strong impression on me. He leapt up and down, shouting loud Zulu words and we all had a most happy time. Father bought me bead necklaces from the black women in the streets, sitting with all their local crafts by the beautiful, warm Indian Ocean.

We left Durban and drove up to Johannesburg, four hundred miles to Mother and Father's house, and had yet another week in the same fashion. The fancy hotel in Johannesburg at that time was Lutje's Langham Hotel. Mother gave a reception there, where I had to wear my wedding dress and we had the large bottom layer of our wedding cake, which we cut again, as we had done in England. Mother was having her reception for her son, who had been away so long, and this was her way to introduce me to all the large family and many friends. We stood in line and greeted the guests — very formal, and for me a very special day. Music started and we danced. A jolly uncle came and asked me to dance. We danced round and round with breathless abandon until he said, "We'll have to go the other way round, now. I have a wooden leg and it's getting unscrewed, so we'll go the other way and screw it back in again." I discovered later that he was a great joker and had no artificial leg at all; he just wanted me to laugh! It was all such fun.

Came the morning, Father gave us the keys to a beaten up old Dodge motor car and said, "Up north you go, to work in the family business in Venda." All our books and records and everything we possessed was packed into this vehicle, plus whatever Mother thought we might need, and off we went. The one thing she didn't think to give me was a recipe book, and how sorely I needed one! I had only been a nurse and never had worked with a mother in a kitchen, so I could cook practically nothing. The first gift you should give to a new bride who will be living where there is no support system is a good basic recipe book.

We proceded north for about eighty miles, then Cecil stopped the car and said, "Now we put on white coats." "What for?" I asked. "It's so hot, why must must we put on a full-length coat, even though it's cotton?" (The coats were identical to the ones doctors wear.) "You will see," he said. "The dust." We had reached the end of the tarred roads and from now on I would live with red dusty roads, full of pot holes and corrugations. The coats were an essential part of travel, if you wished to arrive in some semblance of cleanliness. Every time a car approached, we held our breath. I spent my life saying to my children, "Car approaching — hold your breath." Then, all together, we would take a deep breath and wait until we had passed the red cloud the other car had left in its wake. One learns to cope with red dust all the time. This is, of course, one of the reasons the clay pots from Venda are so good — the soil in the north is red clay.

South African women always wore correct clothing — dresses, stockings and shoes. Seldom trousers or shorts. There were no such things as jeans. T-shirts were scarce and we certainly never wore them. My little son grew up even in the bush in proper button-up shirts and bow ties with real lined trousers. My father-in-law wore a suit nearly every day of his life, even in the desert — they were made of cotton, silk, or linen — and he usually wore a buttonhole [flower in his lapel], even if it was only a wild flower. On his head he wore a white pith helmet, a "topee." He was very dignified, like the Victorian era to which we were very closely related.

After driving for some hours we came to a town called Nylstroom. Now I thought I understood why the early Voortrekkers called this place after the river Nile: I, too, felt I must be somewhere near the top of Africa, so far had we travelled. (*Slow* was the operative word!) We travelled on and on, passing many more small places. In between, there was no electricity, just empty black space. It was dark by now — we had travelled three hundred miles.

The last place was called Louis Trichardt, after one of the very early pioneers. I was getting quieter and quieter and quite apprehensive. For those first two weeks, I had been quite sure I had married the right man, but now I was beginning to wonder. In England it would be difficult to head in one direction, keep going, and not fall off into the ocean. I was learning how vast this land is. At this last halt Cecil said,

"This is your last stop. Is there anything you need? And please go visit the toilet." That shook me. No man in England ever would advise you to go to a toilet. But he did because he knew there wouldn't be another, and I couldn't have known. This freedom of speech was something else. On long journeys in broad daylight I remember many times, travelling with my very proper in-laws, that Father would stop the car and say, "All out. Gentlemen look to the west, ladies to the east"! There was probably no tree in sight, so he made it possible for us to have some privacy. Very sensible.

I noticed that Louis Trichardt was made up of one cross street [intersection] with a robot [traffic light] as its only excitement and small local shops lining the two streets. Cecil told me to go and buy anything I might need, as it would be a long time before I came here again. I walked into the chemist [pharmacy] and tried to think of future needs — make-up, creams, etc. I didn't really know what to buy, so I went back to the car and we were on our way. Now it was really dark and there were no lights, just more pitch black bush.

We travelled for another hour and reached the bottom of a long range of mountains and climbed slowly up and up, to the top — to the small village of Sibasa, then the capital of Venda. There are two streets, in an L-shape, and our trading store is at the end of the short street. The police station was at the corner point of the two streets, and up a long sloping main street were all the government buildings, the magistrate's court, and the home of the South African Government Native Commissioner, as he was then known. It was a community of about two dozen whites and 250,000 BaVenda (as the people of Venda are called). In the Venda language the capital was called Tshivhase. The police sergeant was white and all the policemen mixed black races — quite a few Zulus. Sometimes there were also two white policemen. Opposite the police station was the second trading station — there are always two, to keep a fair control on prices and healthy competition. Our opposition (the other traders) were Germans who had been there even longer than we. At that time, Venda was under the South African government. It was only in 1979 that they chose to take independence and govern themselves.

INTRODUCTION TO
VENDA

Our store was made of corrugated iron walls and roof, so it was very hot in summer and very cold in winter. The red dust was everywhere, and with every passing vehicle it rose up in clouds. Across the street from us was an open marketplace, where anyone could bring fruit and vegetables or anything they had to sell. There were four small cells built on the roadside, where any prisoners were housed, but during the day the prisoners were used for fixing the roads or cleaning gardens. We had little real crime and there was no stigma attached to a spell in prison. In fact, if you were poor and hungry it paid you to have a spell as a prisoner, as you were well fed and had someplace to sleep.

Past the store we drove down a long avenue of blue gum trees and silky oaks that Mother had planted in 1935, and into lush green grounds with two houses — one, where Cecil's brother and his family lived (after eight years, they were leaving and theirs was to be our house), the other for cousin Tom, who also worked in the store. His house was where Mother and Father had lived and where Cecil and his brother had grown up.

The trading station was a family business. My sister-in-law, Nancy Graham, whom I grew to love very much, welcomed me and showed me round. Jesse, her husband — a large, happy, noisy man — fills a room with his presence. He and Cecil hadn't seen each other for about five years, and they had much to catch up on. Jesse and Nancy had two little children and were obviously pleased at Cecil's marriage, so that they could leave and start a new life somewhere else.

I told Nancy I would go and unpack but asked, first, "Where's the bathroom?" She said, "Do you want to wash or do you want a toilet, because the toilet is not in the house." Into the garden, around the back, down a stone path was a small house [an outhouse] — a new experience in my life. No water-borne sewerage. (No electricity anywhere, either — I had already seen the paraffin lamps on the tables.) In the little house was a forked stick, handy in case there was a snake inside. Nancy said to me, "I'll wait outside for you." I had a torch [a flashlight], but I said, "Please don't go away" — I was very nervous. There was a wooden seat with a hole in it, and a framed wire mesh that came down over the hole (to keep the insects out; otherwise, bees and wasps could make a hive down the hole). Nancy called out, "I'm just going up to the house for a minute. You'll be all right." The door closed with a loop of string over a nail. I was sitting there quietly, thinking to myself, What have I done? We are miles from anywhere, with few facilities, when I heard some feet coming. A hand undid the string loop and opened the door, and there stood a gentleman. "Oh," he said. "You must be Cecil's new wife." I said, "Yes. Hello, who are you?" "I'm your cousin Tom," he replied, and with that he closed the door, replaced the string on the nail and went away! (The door could be opened from the inside or outside, as it was not a close fit. It didn't offer much in the way of security, but the spaces around it did serve to let in the sunlight and air.) I burst out laughing, as it really was quite funny.

I took the torch and the stick and went back into the house, where a party had started — all the family and friends to welcome us. All the people there knew the Graham family very well because of the length of time the Grahams had made their home there. All Cecil's school life he had been away at boarding school, but he regularly came back on long holidays until the day he joined the army. I was going round the room being introduced to everyone, and there was cousin Tom. "This is Cecil's new wife," Nancy told him. "Yes," he said, "we've met." "That's not possible; she's only just arrived from overseas," replied Nancy. "You tell them," Tom said to me. "You tell them how we met." "Oh, no, no!" I exclaimed, much too shy. It was a long time before I let on about our first encounter!

We had just the one outhouse toilet for the two houses. After I'd been there a few years I decided this was nonsense and that a new toilet was very much my priority, even though the old one was in good condition from a health point of view. But we women also wanted one for ourselves, for each house — which we got for Christmas.

To build such a convenience, you dig a deep rectangular pit about twelve metres deep and build a small structure around it with the wooden seat over the hole. Then you throw down a fresh sheep's head or a large raw liver, shut the door and leave it for a week or two — time for the bugs to develop. These little fellows will devour all refuse and keep things sweet smelling. Once a year I would throw down another liver, just to keep things going. Very efficient, very cheap, no water required.

The whole first week after I arrived in Sibasa there were functions for me to meet everyone. I remember Father giving a party for the black people. (He and Mother had arrived a few days after we did.) A headman stood and made a speech, welcoming Cecil back from the war, and he asked how much Cecil had paid for me. Cecil said "seven shillings and sixpence," [$1.50] which was the price of the wedding certificate in England. The tribal people couldn't understand why he had bothered with someone so cheap. At that time, an ordinary girl in the village cost about £30 [$120], and a girl with royal blood or good family connections was £100 [$400]. So you can imagine that I was really a non-starter! There was an old blind man, there, who wanted to meet me. They brought him forward and he felt me from head to foot. I felt very strange at the time. I couldn't speak much to most of them, as only a few of the women went to school. My servants were all males, because at least they could speak English.

My sister-in-law took me everywhere in that week: "There are the cows; those are yours, and the ducks and chickens. That is the compound, and on Mondays two women come and build a big fire, there, and boil water and do the laundry in these large tin baths." There was a wooden table with a blanket and sheet on it and solid irons placed on the fire to heat them — this for the ironing. Even though it all looked so primitive, all our clothes were beautifully cared for.

The cows were strange to me; I'd never really met a cow before. But they were very necessary, as there was nowhere to buy milk. "Bread?" I asked. "What about bread?" "Oh, you make your own," Nancy said. I nearly died. I had no idea what went into a loaf of bread.

We lived on biscuits [crackers] for the first three months, as I made my first, sorry attempts at making bread! Cecil had some good laughs; I was mortified.

During that first week I met my cook, Phineas, and my house-man, Pete. In the garden I had a gardener and two boys who helped him. It was a large property — 2.5 hectares [6.25 acres] — like a park, with huge trees covering the ground with much-needed shade — somewhere for us to sit and for the children to play. At the far end, I later planted an orchard, with lemons, pawpaws, avocado pears, oranges, and Cape gooseberries.

Another young boy took the cows out every day into the open bush, where they could find food, and of course down to the river for water. Each evening he brought them home and milked them for me. Once a month, the cows were taken to a special dipping area where they were driven through to kill off lice and ticks and other bugs.

Then there was another boy to look after the ducks and chickens and a man who every day took the three-ton truck and filled it with 44-gallon drums and went down to the river to fetch our water. Our house had a tin roof and on each corner stood a large rainwater tank that caught all the rain. This was the best water ever. We used to boil it and sometimes add minerals. The river water was for bathing and washing and everything else. The rain water was the only drinking water we had. You never just drank water, anywhere; you asked for water that had been prepared, to make sure it was safe. I had a bath with taps that were connected through the wall to a drum outside, filled with river water and standing up high on a platform. Underneath the drum, each day, a young boy would make a fire. That provided the hot water so I could bathe everyone. Sometimes there was red clay in the water. When my children were in napkins [diapers] they were often pink, not white.

All in all, I had about nine servants. The time came when Nancy and Jesse and their two children left, Cecil went to work up at the store, and suddenly I was alone with not another white face nor anyone to talk to. The black women were not companions, then, because we couldn't converse, and I was suddenly faced with the reality of my new life. All the staff came to me for instructions, and of course they took advantage of my ignorance and had great fun with me.

The house was built from stones found in the area, as bricks were not easily available. A great verandah went all round, to keep the house cool, and it was gauzed [screened] to keep the insects out. The front verandah was where we sat and had tea and lived most of the day. On the side verandah you could sleep on a hot night, or we played table tennis there. The back verandah was a work place, next to the kitchen.

I didn't have to furnish the house at all. It was as it had always been, with Mother's things. When she left to go live in Johannesburg she bought all new furniture for their new home and left what they had had in Venda. Imagine getting married and having all your wedding presents money because we needed it so much. We had just the few small gifts we had brought with us from England. The house where we lived — and everything in it — was not mine, but the family's. Even the sheets and blankets, the knives and forks and pots and pans. They all belonged there. I was the new item.

We were so lucky to start like that, with so much help. Everything was old fashioned but substantial. I was very grateful and didn't give it a lot of thought, actually. I just moved into the shoes of the previous Graham women. But I didn't have their ability — I had to start from scratch, on my own. Cecil was not there to assist; he was back working flat-out in the store, trying to remember the language again, and the price of goods, and how everything worked.

The trading station was a big business. We were not only traders but also wholesalers, assisting the small black businessmen to buy and cost goods that they would take far away to their villages and make themselves a living. We bought in bulk so that we could assist those men to buy in very small amounts. It saved them transport, also. There were many donkeys, then — a cheap way for them to move their goods through the hills and valleys to the more inaccessible places.

Venda was a large, sprawling country — about eighty miles wide and 120 miles long — in those days. It is much bigger, now, as the South African government purchased white land and gave it back to the Venda people. We were the largest centre, though really so terribly small; beyond us was the low veldt with missionaries, schools, churches, and just huts.

The Grahams have always given a teaching service in trade: If you buy ten pencils, they cost so much; you sell them for so much more and your profit is that. There were scores of little stores all over the countryside, but more there were of hawkers, selling on the roadside. Now there are thousands of hawkers everywhere.

Hawking is in my being. I got to know these people and many became my friends. When, many years later, I became a member of Local Government, protecting them was one of my first battles. I was the Councillor who changed a government ordinance to allow hawking to become legal in Johannesburg. Since I achieved that, many cities and other areas contacted me and have followed suit. This is why the blacks call me "the bridge" because I know and am aware of so many things in their daily lives that most whites don't know. That's what I gained living among them.

I soon saw the pattern of Cecil's life and that I must be a support system for him. Can you imagine, as a bride, that you get your new husband for breakfast, morning tea, lunch, afternoon tea, and dinner, seven days a week with only small breaks in the routine? The relationship either cracks or grows very strong. We have been married nearly forty-four years, and with many ups and downs, having weathered much, we are still strongly married today. But I must say that back then, it drove me dilly sometimes. I had to think up plans to vary the monotony. You run out of jokes and conversations because you know each other completely and have no new, outside stimulation. No television, and the radio was very poor — you had to kneel down close to hear the news. I had a wind-up gramophone for my 78 rpm records. (Long-playing records didn't exist. There were many record changes in a short Mozart concerto.) No tapes or FM frequency or variety.

We had brought with us, as our main luggage, a tin trunk of books, so we read a lot and we exchanged books in the village. We had all my medical books, all Cecil's university books, and lots of literature, so I had two important things: a library of all the great poets and writers, and time. With Cecil to teach me, I slowly absorbed this wonderful material, something that probably would not have happened if we had lived in a city, where so much is available.

As we settled in, the pattern of our life was very pleasant. Cecil had said to me, "I want to help you, now, to educate you. You have the ability; you just never had the opportunity." So that's what happened. He would choose a book for me to read — Shelley was one of the first poets — and then I would read it and we would discuss it. After all, I had an Oxford M.A. as a teacher. So for ten years, my husband taught me — how to read, how to understand music, how to speak, how to dress. We had many differences but it didn't matter. Inside, I so wanted to know all of that. He was my source, and he wanted to give it to me. We loved each other, and we knew each other's strengths and weaknesses. This is how I was introduced to Shakespeare, and today we are both active members of the local Shakespeare Circle in Johannesburg.

Cecil helped me in another very important way, as well. I was born with my head on one side, with my left ear joined to my shoulder, so my head wasn't up straight. I was like that until I was five years old, when my father was away doing some long distance truck driving and my mother had an opportunity to help me. She was very courageous, knowing my father would do nothing for me and didn't want her to, either. She and I walked a long way, to a hospital not near home. When she was asked if she had his permission to do the operation, she said, "Oh, yes, but he's away right now." She told them to go ahead with what was quite a difficult operation at that time. A nurse donated the required skin for the skin graft I needed on my neck and shoulder.

My mother was determined that I was going to have a chance in life and not live like my Auntie Alice, a hunchback. So she took that decision alone. When they asked her to get my father's signature on the anaesthetic form, she told them, "I can't; he's a long-distance truck driver and he's away on a long trip." That was true. He was driving trucks because the Depression years had started and there was no factory work. Normally he worked in the Bristol Aeroplane factory, as a jig and tool maker.

Of course the day came when he returned and was very cross. He hunted for me but fortunately arrived too late. The operation was done. I stayed in hospital for about a year, as slowly my neck muscles became stronger. My head was in a plaster cast like a hood, right down my neck to my shoulders. As I grew it had to be cut off and replaced with a new one — a most unpleasant experience. They cut off all my hair before the new plaster was applied, but of course it grew and it used to itch terribly. They gave me a basin of cold water and a spoon, and I used to dip the spoon in the cold water, push it up under the plaster and scratch, in order to take away the irritation. I remember that every time they cut it off, they used to take a thruppence piece, which was eight-sided, stand it on end and say to me, "If you don't cry we will give you the money." I used to fix my eyes on that coin and make myself quiet, in order to win it.

Luckily for me, living in England where it was mostly poor weather, it was not necessary to expose my neck, so people didn't know. It was very discoloured and brown all my youth, because I was far too shy to let anyone see it. When I met Cecil and realised that we were going to marry, I obviously had to tell him. I had always worn dresses with high necks and lace collars. I told him I was born deformed and he said, "Well, you look all right to me," so I showed him my neck and shoulder. He said, "It's nothing, just a bit of brown. Don't worry." However, he must have thought about it a lot, and he realised that I was very sensitive about it, and he knew I was going to live in an African climate where I wouldn't be wearing cover-up clothing. When we got to Sibasa he said, "We are going to get your neck right, whilst we're here. There are so few people here, no one is going to worry about it. You are going to sunbathe in the garden and let the sun help the skin." Within a year it came right, and now you cannot see anything really wrong, except when I wear earrings — my ears are not level. But most people don't even notice that. Living in a small place certainly helped me overcome that slight handi-cap. But every time I had a baby, my first question as it was born was not, "What is it, boy or girl?" My first question always was, "IS ITS HEAD ON STRAIGHT?"

My eldest daughter, Felicity, was born with a big lump on her left shoulder, with blood vessels (capillaries) in it, so it was quite blue. When I asked the doctor, "Is her head on straight?" he said, "It's a little girl." I asked again, "Is her head on straight?" and he said, "Yes, but there's a growth on her shoulder." I learnt it could be treated and replied, "That's fine; Thank God." It was treated with deep x-rays.

EARLY DAYS

Along the way I learnt how to make bread. I learnt about the cows. I prayed that people would get sick so that I could be useful. I taught the women how to look after their babies. I was always available, so when anyone came to sit on the back verandah — sitting and waiting — I knew they wanted me. I had a sort of out-patient clinic. In this way, I got to know the people and they got to know me. Even when they weren't sick, sometimes they would come just to visit. That pleased me a great deal. I was building up friends, and that became more and more important to me. It was a real growing time, particularly medically.

One thing I learnt early on: Never ask a black woman has she lost a child; ask her how many. In the circumstances in which they live, only the strong survive. We in the Western world rear the weak as well as the strong. In more "primitive" societies only the strong survive. If they don't lose babies by miscarriage, they often do so in the child's first two years through malnutrition, diarrhea, dehydration, and the like. So, living there, I was used to seeing sick children and to having my own quite sick. I, too, suffered three miscarriages. When you live in a remote area, you do not rush back to the city for everything. It takes time, money, and leaving the store understaffed. Cecil relied on me to make all our medical decisions. But remember, I am not a doctor, only a nurse, and diagnosis is the most important part of any illness, so the pressures on me were quite difficult sometimes. However, I did set up a nursing bedroom in my house, and whenever someone needed care and attention, it was my pleasure to be useful. I was so pleased to be able to use my gifts.

I also informed the BaVenda people that I was available whenever they needed anything. This I enjoyed very much. Don't we all need to be needed? I remember a woman coming in with a large wet tropical sore on her leg. She was wearing the traditional lot of wire bracelets on the leg, covering the sore and rubbing into it. She would not let me take any bracelets off, so I had to clean the sore, treat it, and bind it up with all that dirt and wire still in place. She couldn't speak any English, so my houseman explained to her that I was going to cut the sore and clean it up, and that it would be painful. And that, if she required it, he could hold her still. She needed no help — just sat stoically, accepting the pain.

I remember also helping the white sergeant policeman who was allergic to bees and once bitten gave real problems. One day he was so bad I had six other policemen holding him down in bed because he was in a fit and would have fallen out of bed and injured himself.

My missionary doctor used to give me some medicines which I kept in a special cupboard, and whenever anyone was ill, I would send a runner to the doctor with all my findings — temperature, blood pressure, pulse, general condition, whatever else I had learnt. I would write it out, tell him what medicines I had in my cupboard, and ask what I should do. I could cope quite well at a distance, if the runner got through the four rivers. It was only ten miles or so by road to the mission station but one talked in rivers, up there, because there were no bridges, then, only causeways made of concrete — fine, in good weather. It was seven river causeways to the nearest town, Louis Trichardt, though it was only fifty miles. Sometimes the rivers were in flood and not passable; sometimes the runner discovered the doctor was out in the district and couldn't be found, when we needed his advice.

One day I remember the missionary doctor coming over for tennis and the rains came down, the rivers in flood, and he couldn't get back. He stayed with us for four days. (We all wore Wellington boots in the wet season because the water ran everywhere and red soil became thick mud. The mud was so bad we used chains on the tyres, if we had to drive in it. When it was really bad, I took up all the floormats in the house so we could sweep the water out.)

I once had my three-year old son unconscious for six days with extremely high temperatures, and I was the only medical person in Sibasa. I once cut open a deep infection in the buttock of one of my little daughters, with no anaesthetic. I got my nanny and houseman to hold her down whilst I cut and cleaned up the wound. She sobbed and sobbed and finally fell asleep. It had to be done; there was no one else to do it.

Opposite my house was an old gnarled fig tree where sat a man called Ralushai, a herbalist. He was always there, for years, and he looked old all the time I knew him. Behind him was the marketplace — two long cement tables, standing under a thatched roof; that's all. Most days, I would walk over there from my house. It was something to do, and I would take a half-hour just to purchase a pawpaw. No hurry; there's nowhere to go, and if you hang around you might see a friend to chat to or something interesting might pass by. I used to stand by and listen, as Ralushai "treated" those who came to him.

From my house, up a gravel path to the store, was about 100 yards, through the compound where the staff lived and cooked in an open kitchen with a tin roof (no sides to it — too hot). Through the compound, past the store and across the red clay road to the market was a walk of about seven minutes. In the compound were huge iron pots where the main food was cooked every day. At 1:00 PM the bell rang, the store closed for an hour, and all our staff — the store men, the lorry [truck] drivers, the outside labourers, petrol attendants, carpenters, gardeners, and all the rest — would gather there and be given a good hot meal. My children always loved visiting there, to be in all the hustle and bustle. We didn't eat in the compound, but we provided everything. Everyone was well fed and very healthy.

Our trading station was like a small village in itself: In our carpenter's workshop they made doors, windows, coffins, and some furniture. We had a petrol station (with a pump handle you physically pumped, as there was no electricity) and a "post office" — in reality, a shoe box! There was a collection desk for dry cleaning (the clothes were sent to Louis Trichardt for the actual cleaning), and we took orders for periodicals and newspapers, which came from Johannesburg.

A huge railway truck with trailer came from town (Louis Trichardt) every day, carrying passengers and goods. Everything came in that vehicle — it was our lifeline. It stopped all along the way from town, delivering at any point, so it arrived in Sibasa nearly always after our evening meal. We would hear the noise and the shouts of men in the compound "Railway!" — so Cecil knew he had to go up and unlock the storerooms and check the goods. If ever I purchased something through a newspaper advertisement, there was always the great excitement of waiting for it to arrive on the railway truck.

I once bought a large sideboard — my first new piece of furniture that was mine — and everyone in the village came to see this beautiful new asset. It arrived one night in a crate on the railway truck and cost £75 [$300] — a great deal of money, when you realise Cecil was earning £10 [$40] a month, but of course we had a free house and no living expenses. Each night I asked Cecil, "Anything on the railway truck for me?" and there would be a great sense of expectation.

Once a month I received a brown paper parcel from Thrupps, in Johannesburg — my bacon and cheese in a soggy oil mess because of the heat and the many days in transit. But it was very welcome, because I couldn't get it anywhere else. Once a week there was a roll of newspapers — many days old, but it was news. I used to read about all the shows and concerts going on in the big city and envy all those attending such delights.

Within one week of our arrival there was a sale in the house of some government officials who were leaving, so it meant that things were available with no transport difficulties or costs. Government officials only stayed for set periods in their careers and then moved on to somewhere else. Cecil went down to see what there was and bought me a sewing machine — a table machine with a handle that turned to operate it (remember, no electricity). He paid £18 [$72] for it and it was a beauty, with silverwork on the table part. I asked, "What's *that* for?"not being at all domesticated at the time. It was not my idea of a present. Later, of course, it became my most useful tool and I loved it. Sadly, I lost it in a house fire many years later.

There were no clothes for sale in our store, only cloth. One day Cecil came down from the store with a roll of floral material, trying to encourage me to sew. "Thought you might like some new curtains," he said. Of course I did learn and made them and then never stopped sewing. I made a lot of my own clothes and some for him and a lot for my children. I was never very good, but I did try. The other ladies in the village helped me and showed me everything. At one of their tea parties, in the early days, they were all sitting with some work in their hands and one of them said, "Don't you do any handwork, Rae?" I said, "No, I don't." I was the only wife there who didn't. But it was only a matter of time before I was knitting, embroidering, and sewing — even making tapestries.

It was inevitable that I would learn to create things, as when I came to Johannesburg once a year to shop I had to anticipate all the family's needs plus the needs of friends getting pregnant (or myself, for that matter!) and things I would want to give for birthdays, Christmas, and other celebrations. It was simpler to buy "the makings," rather than actual things; then one could make the items as the need arose. Lots of white wool [yarn] was essential: All the babies wore white; even the little boys wore white gowns until they walked. My babies all wore embroidered gowns with lace and pretty ribbons.

All the functions and parties included everyone, because we were so few, and we all helped to provide the feast. I introduced Christmas as a big holiday there. We used to decorate a truck with coloured paper and balloons, and I made a Father Christmas outfit for one of the older men to wear. In the worst heat of a southern hemisphere December, he would tog up in black boots, an artificial beard, the lot, and — poor man — he suffered in the heat performing for the few children. It started out just for our children and others in the village, then it got bigger and went into black schools. Eventually there was a large black man who became a regular Father Christmas.

I always made a full Christmas with roast turkey, puddings [desserts], carol singing and so on. And how we suffered, eating all that food in such a hot and humid climate! But it was important for me to keep alive the traditions that I related to, and to create them for my children.

It took me about a year to really settle down and belong. On a regular basis I would pack my suitcase, dress for travelling, and be sitting and waiting for Cecil with my hat and gloves on. "Oh, you're leaving, are you?" he would say. "Yes, I want to go back to England," went the conversation. But I never did. It was the set pattern that became boring, sometimes. Every morning I would interview the staff and discuss the day's tasks, then they would all go away and do them, and then I sat — with no handwork at that time — and no one seemed to need me. That first year I hadn't established how I could serve the community, so no one came. I would read, then walk round the garden and watch the gardeners — it was mostly too hot for me to do much — then walk across to cousin Elizabeth, who was quite a bit older than I and was always busy baking, sewing, and doing other things. She was married to Tom, my father's first cousin. Often she would make jam. I couldn't make jam — I soon found out that I could do very little. And so I had nothing to do. Having dressed and packed, I would beg Cecil to take me to Louis Trichardt and give me the money to go back. One day, when Father and Mother were visiting us, Father realised what was going on. As all parents do, they were watching me, and he did a very clever thing: He gave me an envelope with exactly the right amount of money to take me back — one way. It meant that I didn't feel so trapped. I could leave if I chose, but I couldn't come back; there wasn't enough money in the envelope for that. I never used it, because I doubted that I would ever have enough money to return. I put the money into a Building Society [Savings and Loan] book and left it there for many years, until a special occasion arose and I bought an antique silver cake basket — for Cecil.

¥

Years later, when Father died (1954), my cousin Elizabeth and I asked the men if we could now have a task in the store. Father never allowed the women near business, and it was very frustrating and boring for us at times. Immediately a post was created for Elizabeth, running a Building Society branch where the local people could invest their money. There were a lot of schoolteachers and clerks, policemen and labourers who received a cheque each month for their salary. At that time we had a small room set aside where once a week the Standard Bank sent out an official to run an agency service, but this meant that only for a few hours a week could one bank. Elizabeth was wonderful with all the people, particularly the uneducated, to whom she explained why it was good to put the money into their books because of dividend potential. This took a while to explain, but she took endless time to make sure they knew their money was safe and growing. She got to know hundreds of people and they all trusted her. During the war she had run a classy dress shop in York, England, so she understood business, and she was very good at helping people. She would say, "Now listen, Susan, I know you're pregnant and will need money, " or "You are getting married and need to build a hut," or whatever, and then she would advise how to put the whole cheque in but take out only enough to live, and she explained how it would earn interest. She would say, "I'll only give you £2 [$8]; that's enough." "Oh please, Mrs Wood, can't I have more?" someone might ask, and she'd reply, "All right, £2 10s [$5], but that's all; the rest into savings. You will thank me one day." She was like a grandmother to them all, and how they loved and trusted her!

I never handled money for myself — there was no need. I had a small exercise book [notebook] to keep track of my purchases in our store, and at month's end that book was tallied by the men, who made an entry of our spendings. I never carried a handbag anywhere, not for ten years, except on the rare occasions when we went to Louis Trichardt. Then I would dress up with good shoes and bag and go shopping and visiting friends in town. What a treat! In Sibasa I was confined to shopping in one shop — ours. Not that I minded that: We had a good comprehensive range of just about anything.

I did use money when I bought fruit and vegetables from the outside market. Cecil would give me money for that. We didn't barter or bargain; there were set prices.

Stocktaking, in the store, took place at the end of June. The whole family came together in Sibasa, took stock, cost it, and worked out the year's profit. It took about a week, and the whole family worked hard. (We women were not allowed in the store, so we worked with the sheets of figures at home, adding up and cross-checking. Dreary work and hundreds of pages of it.)

It was an extremely busy week. At mealtimes, when we saw the men, we women would say, "We hope it's going well. Are you happy with everything?" (This was the most important time of year for all of us.) And Father — always the perfect gentleman — would reply, "Yes, ladies, it's coming along nicely."

On the final day we would all get together in my house. "Spot" time: whisky, wine, good snacks. Mother baked special things to eat. We all dressed in nice dresses — it was an "occasion." A pile of envelopes would be on the table and Father would tap for attention to make a speech: "I wish to drink a toast to my sons and nephew and all the gentlemen who have been involved in the stocktaking of the year, and to thank them for another good year of business. Ladies, you may now drink a toast to a good year. I add my usual tribute to the ladies for being so supportive of us for the last twelve months, and now we head for the next twelve. Here is my Thank You to each one of you." And we each got a white envelope with cash in it. That was our only "income" for the year. I don't know what Mother got, but we girls all got the same. In the early years it was £100 [$400]. That was a lot of money, and with it I purchased birthday presents and anything I privately wanted. It gave me independence. The first year I didn't know I would get that gift and I had to ask Cecil for every penny. Even when I wanted to buy him a present, he had to give me the money. I disliked that very much. Father was very clever in giving us cash. There was nowhere to invest it and make it into £101 or £102 — the nearest Building Society was in Louis Trichardt, some fifty miles away — so I just kept it in a drawer. I didn't waste it or blow the lot; I saved it. I had never had so much money in my whole life, so it was precious. Of course it was like Victorian times, but I didn't mind that. I was very grateful to be a part of it.

Our life was a nice combination of hard work and play. We had a place in the middle of our village with two tennis courts made of red clay ants' nests, rolled hard, and white powder paint for the lines. Nothing is better to play on than that kind of surface. Next to the courts was a long bench to sit on and a wooden table with a slatted roof over it. That was called "the clubhouse," where we would have tea. We all wore correct whites — fairly long white dresses for the women (no trousers or shorts allowed) and long white trousers or long shorts for the men. We had plenty of labour available, only too glad to get a job, so the courts were rolled regularly and lines were freshly painted every week. We never missed Saturday afternoon tennis. It was social, fun, and some form of exercise. We all played and got quite good. It cost fifteen shillings (about $3.00) for a "ball boy," and they needed and wanted the jobs. It was Father's maxim, "Employ as many people as possible." There were occasions when there were things I well could have done myself, but I was told, "Oh, no; employ someone. They need the work." We would sometimes employ dozens of women just to come in and weed the grass, which was extensive, all over our property. It was pleasant work to them — crowds of friends, chatting to each other as they worked, and at the end of the day, cash in their hands.

The Graham family, by this time, had been in Venda for twenty-one years, so the responsibility we felt to the people was different from those who just came and went. We had a strong bond with the community — and still do, to this day. Father used to say, "You put back where you make a living." He and both sons served on the hospital board and made donations and supported local projects in many different ways. This was our home.

When Father bought the store from an earlier trader, it was made of corrugated iron, because traders could never own the land and were given government leases based on a six months' notice period. Father had upgraded it a little, but it was still the same building when Cecil and I arrived, with no modern facilities. It was very hot to work in, and very dusty. Many years later we built a brand new building, with cement floors that could be washed and regularly cleaned and with a proper ceiling, so it was much nicer to work in.

LIFE IN SIBASA

There were many new things for me to learn about life in Africa, and I found them all fascinating. Around our store were rings of large stones, about ten feet in circumference. Scraping away the soil from inside the ring, you would find a sheet of iron, and underneath that a pear-shaped pit going down about twelve feet. That pit could hold up to three hundred bags of maize [corn]. Around the outside it would ferment and form a crust, so that every bit inside kept fresh, for years if need be. It was like the old Egyptian pits for storing grain, and very successful it was. The soil is hard red clay and so having dug the pit, you set a fire going in it, and it bakes beautifully. What you have is a large, underground clay pot. No one ever interfered with them — there was great honesty in our village. When a drought season came and we needed maize, the pit was opened and left for a while for the gasses to dissipate. Remove the fermented crust, set up a pulley-and-tackle tripod with a bucket on a chain, and you're in business to sell from the pit. Each evening the sheet of iron and a few stones were placed on top — no lock or anything.

One day, I remember, we found a large, very fat donkey in the pit! He had commenced eating, fell in, continued eating all round him, and sunk in deeper and deeper. That made quite a day's excitement, whilst canvas was pulled under his stomach by men who jumped into the maize and helped to get him out with a larger pulley from above.

When we had good rains the crops were excellent and there was much maize. The women would come from all over with large baskets on their heads. The maize was weighed and poured into the pit and they were given a piece of paper with a price on it, which they could take into the store and use as money. It was a good service to the public and it meant that no matter how bad the roads were, in bad drought times there was always plenty of food stored. Whenever they opened up a pit it was a big event, and we all took part in it. The children loved the fun and excitement.

I never locked my house. In any case, there wasn't much point because you just had to break some of the wire gauze on the verandah and tear it off the wooden frame and you were inside. I closed the curtains all day to keep the sunlight out — to keep the inner rooms cool to sit in, in the evenings. On hot evenings you couldn't read near the paraffin lamp: It was too hot — the lamps were hot. There were always insects. Even though there was gauze at every window some still got in, and they used to fly over the lamps and singe themselves. The first thing I ever remember of the night I arrived was sitting on the verandah, watching the gauze. It was covered with insects beating against it, to get at the light. It was alive, and the lizards and chameleons were having a feast eating all this available food. I thought, My God, how savage it all looks. There was a massacre going on out there, and no one took any notice. I thought to myself, Africa is something else.

I remember that night so well. Just the family. "Spot" time. This is a nightly ritual in South Africa, no matter where you are. "Spots" are sherry, whisky, or brandy and little biscuits, peanuts, and cheese. The men always had their whisky and we ladies were expected to have sherry; it was the done thing.

Privacy was another matter — and another lesson. That first week Cecil was very tolerant and understood my unease. I would go to bed and he would stay on and have another drink with his brother, to give me privacy, because I either had to go outside through the orchard to that primitive toilet (primitive to me, anyway!) or use a chamber pot (a "gozunder"!) kept beneath the bed. I was too nervous to go outside in the pitch black, so I chose the latter. I was quietly sitting there when Cecil came in. "Don't come in now; I'm not ready," I said, but he replied calmly, "Now, Lovey, don't get upset, but don't move. There's a problem." Of course I was immediately frightened. "What is it? What's wrong?" "Don't panic. Just don't move." "I'm frozen," I said. It turned out there was an enormous poisonous spider on the rim of the potty, just next to my posterior! Cecil got to it, disposed of it, and all was well. Later, those were things I looked for and disposed of myself.

I had scorpions in my cupboards, snakes in the house, snakes inside boots (I learnt always to shake them out before putting them on), once a boomslang [tree snake] in a pram next to a sleeping baby girl, once a little snake curled up inside my dressing gown [bathrobe] pocket. I always tied mosquito gauze over my prams to keep insects and things out, but sometimes things got in.

When I kept finding snakes in the house, I said to Cecil, "We seem to be getting quite a lot, lately; let's investigate." We had seen quite a few ringhals (a very poisonous snake) on the property and it appeared that one had got in under the kitchen and laid a lot of eggs. Now they were hatching out and going all over the house. We had a shotgun for this purpose, because you need to be very accurate when you shoot snakes. We only shot them immediately round our property, to keep it safe for the children. We never shot them in the bush. There were plenty of snakes around, of many varieties, and most of them poisonous. They are poisonous from the moment of birth, no matter how small they are, and the smaller the person bitten the more deadly the poison, so obviously I worried a lot for my small children. I lost a little dog once, because snakes are quicker than dogs. Not quicker than cats, though. I kept about fourteen cats in the back yard, just to keep down the snakes, and they did. It's quite a sight to see a ring of cats around a snake. The snake doesn't have a chance. I kept the house clean and investigated for snakes on a regular basis, so we would be safe at night. The doors would be open and shut during the day, with children coming and going, so things got in, but during the night the doors were closed.

Whenever the black staff saw a snake they would stand still and scream out, *"NOGA!"* ("SNAKE!") and we whites would react. I had to learn fast what to do, in all circumstances: There were a lot of people in my care. One time, one of the gardener's helpers got spat at by a ringhals, straight into his face. This can blind you. "Quick!" I shouted, "Bring him into the kitchen!" I ran and got a bowl of milk and literally poured it all over his face and eyes. It dilutes and dissipates the venom. He survived unharmed. As I was a nurse, a white, and the madam, it was expected of me to react and supply the support system for them all.

Actually, it was also my pleasure to be useful and caring. There are certain simple things one learns to do. Next to every door throughout my house were bricks, covered with sackcloth. Some of them were embroidered to look nice, but they were there not just for doorstops: Whenever a snake was spotted crawling down a passageway or somewhere in a room, it was easy to pick up that brick and place it on top of the snake to immobilize it whilst you made a plan on how to get it out of the house. I didn't want to frighten houseguests, and I didn't want to bring up my children with fear, but it was nice to know there was a brick handy everywhere.

Our house wasn't flat on the ground. It was built with a large space underneath. On a regular basis we would lift up the wooden floors (constructed with trap doors, easy to lift) and then a group of village children would dig and scour and look for white ants. I paid quite a sum for a queen, because she produced all the little white termites that would eat the timber — the doors and door frames, window frames, and the floors themselves. This timber often had to be replaced, as we had an ongoing battle: us against the white ants. We would do a room at a time. All the furniture into the garden, the floors taken up, and then a real cleaning banging, searching for anything, including ants, snakes, and scorpions. Floors back, furniture cleaned, banged, and polished, and finally a clean, safe room. Then on to the next room. It was a constant task. As I walked round, doing my daily chores, I would tap on anything made of wood. If it sounded hollow, then the ants were inside. That meant the carpenters from our workshop had to come down and replace all the hollow wood. In fact, as I visited other houses I would automatically knock the door frame and advise Elizabeth or whoever that they had white ants. It was part of my life.

Once, a group of our children were playing under the carport — a roof on four poles to shade the cars, with a loose gravel floor. The children were pushing little cars on small tracks they had made, and as I walked past I saw a cobra snake right in the middle of them. I remember there were six children and the eldest was six years old. These children grew up with a wonderful sense of freedom; they ran and played among their three houses, where they were always welcomed. (By this time another cousin had arrived to work in the store and a third house had been built.) They would check on what was cooking in each house and decide where they would eat. We were all their mothers or aunties, so it was a large support family. I knew I could not save all six children from the snake, so I walked on a bit, to think what to do. Oh, Lord, I said, help me. What can I do? Then I had a bright idea: I called out, "Who wants tea with special iced zoo biscuits [cookies]?" The whole six got up and came running to me. I shall never forget how I put my arms round all of them and had very wet eyes. Thank dear God, it had worked. Then I took them all up to the store to buy the promised treat and told Cecil about the cobra, so he could go down and shoot it.

Today children get many treats, every day, but in those days they certainly did not often get iced biscuits, and iced animal biscuits were very special. Hence, the force of that magnet. For those children that was party stuff. I went to tell the other two mothers, and you can imagine their relief. I knew everything was OK, but once it was over I was shaking, having a reaction to the fright. The children never knew. What is so strange is, having been born there, none of them said, "Oh look, there's a snake." They were too busy playing. But I have read somewhere that snakes seem to have an affinity with children. They don't automatically strike, only when threatened. Perhaps if I hadn't walked past just then it would have quietly slid away. Perhaps.

DISEASES AND ILLNESSES

Picnics by the rivers were a common thing we did with the children. When you arrive, the first thing you do is have the adults get out of the car and make some noise, to scare away any crocodiles that may be there on the bank. Once you are sure it is clear, then the children get out and play in the sand alongside the river. There are plenty of crocodiles in the rivers in Venda, and I never let my children paddle.

I obviously became very aware of the diseases there. Bilhartzia is a disease that gets into your bloodstream and then moves all over your body to many organs. It is carried by a snail in all the rivers, and if you put your hands or feet in the water and have a small cut or opening in the skin, this microbe penetrates and enters your body. It is extremely difficult to get rid of, and most blacks suffer from this disease because they are constantly at the rivers.

I had bilhartzia for ten years and couldn't get rid of it until I came to Johannesburg and they had discovered a cure. My husband had it for many years, as did three of my children. It is a most debilitating disease that takes away all your energy. You don't know you have it for quite some time, only as it moves around your body and different symptoms occur. When it is in your lungs you cough and cough. I coughed for about two years. When it finally reaches your kidneys and bladder, then you have blood in the urine. It is a disease that keeps recurring. Every time a black goes into the river for water, he can pick it up again. So it is no surprise to me that people from the tropics, where I lived, were constantly without drive or much energy. Now there are good cures that can work quickly, but in those days we accepted setbacks and didn't rush to Johannesburg just because we didn't feel well. We got on with life. It was the coughing that finally made me do something about it.

The medicine for the cure makes your body bright yellow, like a fever colour, and you lose your balance and stability, so you have to stay lying down whilst you take the cure. When whites in Johannesburg used to complain to me, "My gardener doesn't do much work in a day," I would find out if he came from the north, from Venda, and if he did he probably had bilhartzia. Even if he was recently cured, if he'd been home again on holiday he probably picked it up again. This is one of the sadnesses: There is no immunity.

When I placed my babies outside with nothing but nappies [diapers] on, sometimes bugs would get inside the nappies and lay eggs, particularly if the nappy was wet. Then the baby bugs would hatch out in the warm sun and burrow into the skin of the groin. I remember my first horror, when I changed a nappy and saw small bugs crawling about, underneath my baby's skin. I got a needle and cut open the skin, to get them out. Then I learnt that when the nappies have been washed and dried on the line outside in the sun, it is likely these microscopic bugs are in the nappy. So you must always iron the nappies — and every other garment — with a very hot iron, to kill the bugs. Little things like that you learn as you go.

Tickbite fever also was common. Within two weeks after I arrived in 1948 I had that fever. It comes from a tiny tick bug that hangs in the grass, and as you walk it attaches itself to you and burrows in your flesh. Once it is in your blood you get a high fever and have to go to bed. The bug is a tiny thing, and you must always examine yourself all over if you have been out in the bush. But if you find one you mustn't pull it off: The head will remain and you will get sick. You must take some raw paraffin and dab it on with cotton wool; that kills it and it falls off.

Paratyphoid is there also. Of my family, seven of us got it. It comes from a bug similar to the one that gives typhoid, but the disease is slightly different. There is a cure for it.

Scorpions are common. I had them in the house, everywhere. I remember taking some sheets out of the linen cupboard and finding a scorpion amongst the linen. He fell out onto my chest. Charming. Their bite can give you a bad time.

With my first pregnancy I was so ill I was in bed for seven months, carried from chair to bed to car to chair, very ill and very weak. At that time the Queen of Persia was suffering like me and I read that she had found relief by drinking champagne from the moment she awoke. I didn't have that luxury but I tried port wine, first thing every day, and it worked. I didn't vomit any more and I could eat. I had to tell my missionary doctor that I was literally living on port wine! I was eventually wheeled into hospital in a wheelchair to have my baby, Clive.

My son was bitten by a spider when he was three years old, and he was unconscious for six days. You cannot live with a temperature of 107 degrees, and I knew that. During that week his temperature rose higher and higher until it reached 106.4 degrees. I sat next to his bed day and night, praying and watching, not knowing what was wrong with him. He could hardly breathe. I used to wet my face and lean over him to see if I could feel a breath. It was agonising. He would have contortions and go stiff like a piece of wood. So I placed a large tin bath in the bedroom and lifted him out of bed into the warm water, until the fit would go away and his body was relaxed again. One day, whilst I was doing that, I saw a small pocket of pus underneath one toe. I knew then at last what was wrong with him. He must have been bitten, and he had septacaemia, with poison throughout his whole little body causing the fever. When I found the source of the fever I sent a message to the mission station: "At last I know." You see, one day my son just fell over and went unconscious, and I didn't know what had happened to him. Later I found the spider — and several others — in my kitchen. In that hot climate it was common for us all to run barefoot.

When the doctor got my message, he knew that my son had had septacaemia for six days and that only one thing could help save him: penicillin. But he didn't have any and didn't know where to get any. He left the mission hospital, came rushing over to me and said, "I don't know where to get any, but I'm off and I won't come back until I find some." Fifty miles away was Louis Trichardt — a small place — but 100 miles away was Pietersburg, with a large hospital. He told me to just keep bathing the child until he got back. You can imagine how long it seemed whilst Doctor was gone, and how I prayed. He drove from doctor to doctor, from place to place, until he found some penicillin and drove frantically back.

We then had to discuss how much to give: My son was small, not weighing very much, and he had a fever higher than either of us had ever worked with before. How much to give? We didn't have time on our side, so we had to get it right. If we gave too much we would kill him; if not enough, he would die anyway. We took a guess, the doctor gave the injection, and I sat and waited. During the night, Clive's temperature fell from 106.4 to 96. We had probably given a little too much, and the reaction was very drastic indeed. He must have been quite a tough little boy because he withstood the drastic change, and by about 3:00 AM I could see the worst was over. By 8:00 AM his temperature had levelled out and I knew he was going to make it, though he was still a desperately sick child.

In Louis Trichardt, I later learnt, they had been having night and day prayer vigils for my son. I didn't know it at the time, but much later I found out just how much loving support I was actually getting.

During this time, in the bedrooms next door, I had my husband and my baby daughter (aged 18 months), both with mumps. Outside each of the three bedrooms, I had gowns and masks and scrubbing bowls, so I could keep the infections separate. I was running a hospital all by myself. I used to go from one patient to the other. For a whole week I never really slept — just occasionally had a nap. My husband and baby were quite ill, but I didn't have much time to be very worried about them. My poor Cecil was sure our son was dead, and I couldn't discuss Clive with him because he was so ill too. I was the only medical person in the village, so there it was. I had to make special diets, as my cook didn't know about hospital food. Invalid diets are very important when you have weak patients. If I had had only the baby sick, I would have been busy just with her, but she got better by herself. It is easy to catch mumps. Probably there was a child in our store who was carrying it, and Cecil picked it up there.

When I saw that Clive was getting better I was able to go and tell my husband, but he couldn't believe it. "Are you sure he is still alive? I was sure he was long gone. Please bring him to my bedroom window so I can see him." I said, "I can't. He's alive, but only just; I dare not bring him near your mumps." "And the baby?" he asked. "How is the baby?" "She, too, is alive and will get better. Just give me time." After that I was able to relax a little and just nurse them all. The day came when I could carry Clive to Cecil's window and they saw each other. It was a very moving moment.

I never got sick myself, from the mumps. I think the Lord knew that was too much. There is a limit to how much one person can do.

When Clive started to recuperate he did get the mumps, because he was so weak and vulnerable. I suppose it was inevitable, although I was scrubbing up before seeing each person and was so very careful. He took a long time to get really well and strong again.

MY MISTAKES

I was so happy with our family celebration of Christmas, in Sibasa, I wanted to spread it further and asked Cecil to please let me do Christmas in the store. He told me the village people wouldn't like it, that I was wasting my time, but that I could go ahead and do it if it pleased me. I asked him to give me £20 [$80] to spend on it, thinking that if I lost it all I would put it down to experience — but of course I was hoping I wouldn't lose it all!

I ordered all sorts of things from the travellers — the travelling salesmen. I got to know them all because they would come regularly and have lunch with us whilst spending a half-day showing Cecil their different ranges of goods. Some of them became my good friends and every year at Christmas they would bring me a special cake or some chocolates. I explained that I wanted to sell Christmas to the Venda and asked what they might have. I bought cards and calendars — no trimmings or decorations, as there was no way they were going to decorate a tree. I knew the whites would come and buy and fill in with what they needed and I told Cecil I wanted to do it all — even the selling — by myself. That was something I'd not been allowed to do before.

He gave me a place at the counter where I set up my little display, and all my black friends came and asked what I was doing. "Something different," I said, and had such fun explaining all about our cultural behaviour. "What's that, Mrs Graham? What's that for?" they would ask.

I knew the cards would never sell in packets, so I split them up and tried to sell one card at a time. "Now, you know it is Christmas," I would explain. "Well, this is what we do. We buy these cards for our friends and write loving messages to them and either deliver them or send them by post." I would read the whole inscription inside the card and tell them about the Christmas story. "I will help you write in this card, your name and everything, and then you send it to your friend," I told them.

One man thought this was great and he bought a card. I helped him laboriously write inside and he was ready to send it by child. (I had advised him not to bother with posting his card, as it was quicker and cheaper just to deliver it. By this time the Grahams had built a nice red brick building opposite our store, which we rented out to the Government. It was a smart new post office, with a house attached, for the postmaster. I remember the first postmaster's wife, because she was my age and had a baby, so we became friends. She used to keep a baboon chained to the tree near her baby's pram, to keep watch over the baby. It became quite vicious and once bit my little son. In any case, the "shoebox post office" in our store came to an end and the new post office rapidly became a large and successful one, covering the whole region.)

After a while, he thought about it and asked, "How will I get my card *back*?" "No, no," I said, "you don't get it back. Your friend will send one to you." "But how will he know he has to do that?" he questioned me. He had a point: There was no way that friend was going to know. So because of the problem of the card going away and the purchaser not getting it back, I didn't sell very many. But it was fun and a busy exercise for me, for a short while.

Across the street in the marketplace I had three very dear friends whom I regularly visited: Ralushai, the herbalist; an old man who was so good with metal he bought sheets of it from our store and made tin trunks and boxes; and a third old man who made metal jewellery — bracelets for the arms and legs. The bracelet maker would take a piece of grass and measure your arm or leg and then have the exact circle size. I would choose the wire — fine tin for the bracelet ring itself, then large wire cut up into small metal beads of copper or brass, hammered onto it in beautiful patterns. He would make four of these bracelets for twenty pence. All that time and labour not costed in, just a small profit on the wire itself. I had hundreds made, because my daughters and I all wore them, many of them. The Venda women wore them from the ankle right up the leg and from wrist to elbow. In African society, articles talk. These bracelets say, "We are the people of metal; we are advanced metalworkers."

And so, another idea was hatched: I started with this old man and the women and set up a business enterprise. I got very excited and thought how I could help them to enlarge their businesses and grow very successful. I bought myself another tickey (thruppence) notebook and went to the store and purchased small glass beads in many sizes and colours. I showed the women the sort of patterns that would sell with whites and I chose the colours. At that time we did not wear the very bright colours the Venda women did, and our colour combinations were different as well. "Now," I said, "you make ten necklaces each. Here are the beads, and I will pay you so much per necklace. You will not have the problem of selling them; I will send the whole lot down to Johannesburg, and there you are. They need 100 necklaces: That's how they buy, wholesale."

Great. They started coming to my house and the work commenced among much noise and talking friendship. I thought it was great fun, and the items started coming. I served them tea and biscuits and it was one more day for me, organised with work. "What a business," said Cecil. "You don't cost in your overhead." But I didn't care — it was mainly for the fun.

Actually, Cecil was delighted that I was using my initiative to make a full life and not be bored. But after some weeks, the women stopped coming. In ones and twos they gave up. I would ask after different women and there were always excuses. "It is such hard work," they said. I replied, "It's not hard work. You sit and chat and just create. It's fun and you will make money. Here I am, sorting out the beads and colours for you and assisting you in every way, to help you to produce large numbers, and making tea. I thought we were having a good time." "No," they said. "It's making one hundred of them. It is so much hard work." "But as soon as it is finished I will give you a lot of money." "We don't think we want that much money," they told me. The commitment was too much, too demanding. No matter the reward it wasn't worth it to them. So that was one more lesson I learnt: Do not impose Western concepts, yet. They didn't want the restraints.

I took the beads back to the store. Most of the necklaces were half finished — a complete failure. The year was 1950; too soon.

Likewise, I had gone to my wire bracelet maker and asked him for 100 bracelets in various patterns, with the same idea: I would buy them from him, wholesale, and send them to Johannesburg. He wouldn't have to worry about finding customers in Sibasa. I explained about wholesale pricing, that because he was selling so many direct to me I must have a slightly better price. "No, no, no," he told me. "Because 100 is so much more work I must charge you much more than anyone else. The work is very heavy for 100 bracelets." He wanted a great deal more money, and I had already done a costing down in Johannesburg, so it wouldn't work. One more complete failure. This is why I often say that conceptions and assumptions are very often wrong. People don't look at things the same way. He also said to me, "I'm happy making a little money every now and then. I don't want to have to make a lot of money which I don't need." He was very poor, by our standards, but by his he had everything he needed. His greatest joy — for him and for the other two men as well — was when I took over a packet of lemon cream biscuits for a treat for them. What I call a "just because" present. No real reason. After this I thought to myself, What am I trying to do here, imposing my thinking and my beliefs on a people who are not happy to accept them? "Stop trying to make money for them," said Cecil. "They all eat quite well. When the rains come there is plenty of food — corn, manna down in the low veldt, lots of fruit and veggies and wild things." My pressures on them weren't necessary; they were aggressive intrusions.

MEDICINE
AND THE CLINIC

T here was a life-size picture of a human being outside our store, pasted on a board and numbered all over. If you had a pain in region #4, you came into the store and purchased the medicine in bottle #4. These patent medicines were made of good old-fashioned remedies, known for years among both whites and blacks. They could do no real harm, as there were no poisons among them. As a nurse, I was fascinated — and a little worried. I asked Cecil about them and he said they had always sold them and had never had any problems. They were made in the Eastern Province by a reliable company which made druppels [medicine drops] and lotions and creams. One day, when we went for a seaside holiday with our children, I went to the factory to check on these medicines. The manufacturer was most happy to show everything to the store owners who sold his products, and it was wonderful to see all the components and natural substances they used.

Of course I used many of these patent medicines, myself, for our whole family. Chest complaints are very common in Venda, with the damp, humid, tropical heat, and my children would cough and cough, all night, with great difficulty. All of us owned little tin lamps for such problems: Methylated spirits burned in the base to heat a thick, black syrup that gave off a strong- smelling fume, when it burned, and made breathing easier.

The missionary doctor, from the Donald Fraser Hospital twelve miles away, came every Thursday to spend the whole day in our little clinic. He always had lunch with us and we became very close friends. That mission set up a large church and schools, and the ladies from

Scotland would come out to live and work with and for the Venda people. What good and dedicated folk they were. I loved them all, though I didn't see them very often. When you live miles apart on dreadful roads you can't keep visiting each other, but they were there and certainly we entertained from time to time. There were dinner parties, birthdays, and of course Robbie Burns' birthday, when they would make a haggis and bring it over and we would have a real party. (As Cecil gave a toast to the haggis, he would say, "I understand why it was necessary to invent whisky. It's the only way you can get haggis down!") None of the missionaries drank, but they would laugh. We read Burns' poetry and famous speeches, and this was an important event, each year.

One year, Cecil and his brother decided to improve the medical services and they built a brand new clinic with a little house attached for Nurse Penina — a Venda woman — who lived there permanently and looked after all the patients between Thursdays. She also delivered babies. When the doctor came, he took any really sick patients back to the hospital. In an emergency, we could phone him through the police station and he would send over an ambulance. We called the new clinic "The Cecilia Johanna Clinic" after Cecil's mother, and we gave it to the tribe. I had, by then, thrown aside all my white attitudes to the Venda and decided to learn about their culture, instead, which is what I do all the time, now.

Often, Nurse Penina would come to me and say, "I've got to go up the mountains to someone. Whilst I'm away, will you keep an eye open for me?" It was my pleasure; I actually enjoyed it. When someone needed me and I could deliver a baby or fix a wound I was happy. I remember when Penina delivered twins, and I was so grateful they were both allowed to live. It was not always so, as tribal people are superstitious of twins. The first twins Doctor delivered he kept alive, much to the family's dismay. They are grown women, now, and openly showed their love for him, for having saved them both. "Watch," he had told the family. "These babies will grow up and serve the Lord and show you that twins are not evil." And of course that is exactly what happened: They became super women.

Some of the tribal traditions and beliefs are impossible for us to accept or understand. One night I heard the most dreadful sound of someone in extreme pain, and in the morning I enquired what it was. A woman in the village wanted to become a *sangoma* (another type of witchdoctor) and had been told there was only one way to become really strong: Cut the heart out of your daughter, but do not kill her first. Can you imagine that kind of death? Terrible indeed. It upset me greatly, and I've never forgotten it.

My first aid and nursing life continued, but I was also keenly watching the local scene, to learn what I could. Whenever people were ill, they seemed to buy a white cockerel or a black goat, and when I asked what they needed them for, they would say only, "Oh, someone is sick." I started asking Ralushai, my herbalist friend across the road, many questions. He explained that if the illness was small the chicken would do, but that if it was a big problem then it must be a goat. They are used in the ceremony surrounding the treatment, but the meat belongs to the doctor. I saw these sorts of preparations, but I was never allowed to attend the functions. I kept asking, but no.

HARVEST FESTIVAL

L ying in bed at night I would often hear the beating of drums, and I would try to imagine what was happening out there. I was fascinated and perhaps a little apprehensive at the same time. We were on top of a mountain, and the sound carried far. It also seemed more mystical in the dark. Occasionally I would hear them quite near — within a half-mile — and quite a lot of drums. I learnt that a lot of drums meant something important, a special function of some kind. I would talk to my staff and ask what was happening, but they would tell me nothing. "I want to go. Can I go?" I would ask. "I don't know," was the only reply. I persisted: "Whose village is it? Who is the headman?" But still no response. No help to me at all. I asked Cecil about going. "Oh, I don't know," he would say. Not that it wasn't safe, but that perhaps I would be an intrusion.

In the beginning it was tricky. I was nervous and didn't know the different constraints — where I could tread or sit. Nobody gave me any indication. Although Cecil had grown up there, his mother had not visited the huts in the outlying areas, so this was a first. Nor did any of the other white women go out alone into the black homes: What for? We didn't discuss my going; they just accepted that I was British and different, I guess. I would walk the little red mud paths all over the district and see so many different things. I'd stop everywhere, go in and see a new baby, a woman making pots, someone ploughing with oxen or planting seeds or hoeing the lands. I saw them making baskets, carving wooden dishes, cooking all sorts of things, making beer out of corn mealies (a thick, white, sour drink, but very nutritious, full of vitamin B). There was so much to see and learn, and I was slowly recognised and accepted.

The drums played often, and I started to follow them. One day there was a loud insistent drumming about three-quarters-of-a-mile away, and I set off to explore. I was really lucky because I knew the headman of this particular place and he welcomed me. There was a special ceremony taking place — only for married women, so I was able to actually take part in it. It was Harvest Festival, a Thank You to the gods through the Ancestor Spirits for the past rains and all the crops. To say thank you for fertility you must be married and fertile, and you sing on behalf of the whole community. I was married and obviously very fertile, as I had a baby nearly every year, so with great excitement they tied the rattles around my legs and we started to dance in a circle — about twenty women. In the middle were two solo dancers, the leaders, one with a stick with rattles on it, the other with an axe and a cow's tail. These two were shaking and chopping and sweeping (cutting up and sweeping away the rubbish and mistakes of the past year, a symbolic cleansing process). The rest of us simply danced, and our legs made lovely rattle sounds as we stamped on the ground.

There were two fires. Around one the drums were placed, faces to the fire to tighten up the skins and keep the drums in tune. The fuel for this was hardwood, which burnt slowly and made good heat. The other fire — made with chaff from the mealie lands — was for cooking and providing food for the dancers, who would tire and fall down and sleep or drop out and eat. Others would come and go, but there was constant drumming, singing and dancing until the prescribed Thank You time. This went on, continuously, for twenty-one days and nights.

Rain, in Africa, brings food, but it also brings leisure time. When you are starving or hungry you have no time or energy for celebrations and music. All your resources, money, and time are used for survival. When it rains, then life itself improves. The granaries are full, so there is money to spare — for more bracelets, for blankets, money to go and attend functions and buy the local beer. The dancers are saying, in their dance, "Thank you for fertility, thank you for life itself. We the fertile women, the makers of the children, we are saying, 'Pula, Pula'." (Rain, rain; thank you for rain.) Pula is a thank you for the very fabric of social life. Ceremonies take place that you never see in drought times.

The one great ceremony that takes place at Harvest Festival is the one where a great black ox or cow is killed and the ancestors are prayed to for rain. So this was a great festival, of much joy, and I regularly visited it and danced and became a real part of it. At night I would lie in bed and hear the drums and visualise my friends and their festival. This was one of the first ceremonies I learnt about. Only women and girls were present. No boys or men ever saw it, including my own husband and son.

I attended that function many times over its three-week period. I'm a good dancer and I like to take part. I would take my two little girls, Colette and Felicity (the others weren't born, yet) and place them high up in a tree, where they could see everything nicely and be quite safe. Then I would get my rattles and join the dance. When it came time for food, I ate and trained my children with only one rule: Do not eat anything that is not inside something; then you will not get sick. This means we didn't hurt anyone's feelings and could be quite at ease. The sort of foods that were fine were bananas, oranges, ground nuts [peanuts] in their shells, mealies cooked on the cob in their leaves (we do not strip off the leaves but leave them on for boiling, as they give a better flavour), anything in a covering. Never drink water anywhere except at home, where I boil it. You can't keep saying No to people; that kills love. There have to be lots of Yes's, and this way of eating allowed us to join in.

The set of drums for the Harvest Festival would be the bass voice ngoma, the tenor voice thungwa, and three higher voice murumba. I play the murumba — not well, but well enough to take part in ceremonies. Blacks have good acute ears and can hear if an instrument is out of tune, so they regularly place the skins to the fire, to tune them. If you are driving through my country and see some drums lying facing the sun, then you must know that tonight there will be a ceremony. I always stopped at such times, made a small camp, and waited for the function. I was never disappointed. Africans are very musical. From the moment the baby is born it is placed on its mother's back and is carried there for at least two years. From the unborn babe right next to the heartbeat, the born babe is carried again near the heartbeat and is a part of that moving mother. When the mother dances, the child is also dancing; when she plays the drums, the beat is carried to the child, so the rhythms and music are a part of its very being.

It is mainly a woman's function to play the drums. When you see African musicals with a line of male drummers beating away with two sticks, this is not completely accurate. The long murumba is played with the bare hands and practically always by women. The tom-tom kind of drum is played in north Africa, not in the south.

The women would dance in an anti-clockwise circle around the fire and the drums, each one of us with rattles tied around our legs from the ankles to the knees. These rattles are seed pods — large and round — filled with small dried corn seeds or small stones. As we stamped on the ground, all together, they gave a most satisfactory percussion sound. The two soloist dancers in the centre had rattles both on their legs and in their hands.

At the time of this festival the great granaries are full. You can see them everywhere, with the sun-dried corn piled high. This means at least two years' worth of food is stored. The granaries are made of sticks placed in a circle and plaited walls of sticks and sisal, with a plaited floor above ground, to keep out the insects and mice. When you need to cook porridge (every evening), you take some of the cobs, scrape off the corn, and pound it in a large pounding block with two heavy sticks. Two women pound together, singing mafuwe — pounding songs — to make the work easier. Most Venda men have two wives; the wealthy have many. The songs are simple sentences. First woman: "I have to go down to the river." Second woman: "Ahe, Ahe Will you look after my child?" "Ahe, Ahe." When a Venda speaks or sings it is not to a silent audience; there is always a reply. Ahe means "Yes, I am here, I'm awake, I listen."

After the pounding, the grain — which is now a powder — is placed in a winnowing basket and shaken to let the chaff blow out. The meal is then placed on a woven mat to dry in the sun. It dries and bleaches. The women go down to the river for water and bring it back on their heads in clay pots. I have finally learnt to do this, but it takes practise to carry a pot this way. To walk well with a pot takes a certain posture — with the spine upright and a gentle walk. You take a piece of cloth and coil it into a ring, place that on the top of your head, and the pot sits in the ring. When the pot is full, you break off branches of green leaves, wash them and place them across the top of the pot. Then, as you walk, it will not spill. You get into a rhythm of walking — always in a single long line. The little paths of Africa are narrow; our feet create the path, over time.

Whites, looking at a place of huts and seeing all the cooking utensils lying around, will say, "How dirty." But my Venda women friends said they thought my food preparation was not clean! "We have heard what you do in your kitchen," they told me, "and that's dirty. You take plates from the cupboard and use them as they are; we don't do that. We wash and scour everything as we are about to use it." And they do — each pot, each stick, each bowl or plate. (The cooking of stews and soups, now, in iron pots has created a health problem, with too much iron being absorbed into the body. In the past, pots were made only of clay and food cooked in the fire very well. The iron pots were brought in from overseas, by the early traders.)

A typical Venda home has a hut for the husband and other huts on the side — one for each wife, a teenage hut for the boys, and another for the girls. In the centre is a *kraal* [corral] for cattle or goats. Land is allocated per wife, so the more wives the more land. The wife tends her own land and raises her own crops. She ploughs with a metal blade pulled by an ox. She will dig by hand with an adze, plant the seed, water it, reap it, pound it, and cook it. She makes the beer, and she makes bricks and builds her own house. The husband will make the roof. There is much sharing of work among the wives.

Children are regarded as the insurance for their old age. Years later, when I had staying with me a university-educated Venda man whom I asked what he thought of Johannesburg and everything I had shown him, he said, "Your shame is your old-age homes. You take old people, with all that knowledge and experience, and put them away in boxes. We keep our old with us and ask them for advice. You say you can't live together, with three generations, but all that experience of life is not on tap for you; it's stuck away. We have that experience to call upon — and we do." They have an entirely different attitude to human relationship patterns. The old are their source and fount of knowledge; the best teachers in all the "initiation schools" are old. In my white life I'm considered overweight and getting old, but in my black life I'm nice and round and full of knowledge!

When the Venda husband comes for his meal, the junior wives do all the waiting on him. One will take him a bowl of fresh water, soap, and a towel, so that he may wash where he is sitting. They kneel at his feet whilst he washes. The senior wife will bring the porridge and a special bowl, much smaller, with the relish of the day — caterpillars (very nutritious) or chicken or spinach with onions (moroka), always with salt in it. Maybe, if it's a special day, there might be some meat. It is not often that they eat meat. Cattle symbolise wealth, no matter whether lean or fat. It's the number of them that counts, so they are not killed often. All the beasts are named, and the people know them and call them by name. Each black tribe has a different way to cook the mealie porridge. Zulus make a steamed bread like a large ball; Tswanas make a thick meal porridge; Vendas make a thin, custard-like mixture which is poured into a wooden plate to set like a pancake, with more and more poured and set on top until you have a pile of them. The wooden plate is called an *ndilo*. The husband cuts up the pancakes like slices of cake; you take a slice, peel off the "skin" and throw it to the chickens to eat, then dip your slice into the day's "relish." Delicious!

So everything was prepared absolutely spotlessly clean. Certainly the pots were placed on their sides and the chickens ate the leftovers, but we were eating clean food. One woman reminded me, "You see how clean we are? You do not clean as you use, and you do not take water to your husband's hands. We know; we've asked your servants." They were studying me as I was studying them — but I came short.

All the years we lived in Venda I had to walk behind Cecil, wherever we went, so that he would not lose face in their eyes. I have great respect for tradition; there was no way I would walk alongside him and undermine his authority with the village people. Why did this custom come about? The man walked in front with a stick or spear to protect his wife, who walked behind with the food on her head and the baby on her back. It was a caring custom. In our cities, today, it is often awkward for black men trying to decide how to behave with white women in a lift [elevator]: Does he get out of the lift first or last? How easily we can misunderstand each other's motives. This goes for sitting and standing and words of appreciation, as well: A black person always keeps low down so that his head is never higher than yours — a compliment. And instead of saying "thank you" he will clap his hands several times and place both hands together, which says, "Your gift is so great it takes two hands to hold it." But whites often ask, "Why don't they rise when they are speaking to us and why don't they say 'thank you'?" I could cry, at the misunderstandings.

I teach these other customs everywhere I go. Recently, in front of a school hall packed with white children, their parents, and the governing body, when I was thanked for my speech and the chairman came to present me with a gift, I went down on one knee, clapped my hands twice, and took the gift. Now all those whites saw a City Councillor demonstrate a different cultural pattern, and I hope they will learn and have a better understanding of the other groups in this country. I talk and demonstrate to every group in the city — black, white, Indian, and coloured — so I bridge all four groups, discussing their differences and their similarities. When I do prize-giving ceremonies at the year's end, I have hundreds of young minds I can awaken to their future relationship with other races. You must realise that only in very recent years have the youth of South Africa been able to mix freely; before that they were always cut off from each other.

Communication was not just the sound of drums across the distance of valleys. Every Venda boy carves his own little flute which gives him his own personal note. He keeps that one note as his form of identification. When he wants to contact his friend to see if he's at home, he blows his one note and listens for his friend's note, which he knows, and if he hears it he knows he's at home and he goes totting off to see him. If he hears nothing, he knows he's not there and he saves himself a long trip down a valley and up a hill. Sound is very important in a country where you don't have other forms of communication. Blacks have very loud voices. I have a very loud voice, which is useful in my black life. When you are out walking along a path or a trail and have a long way to go, you don't stop when you pass a group of huts or a village or friends. They shout out and greet you and you shout out and say, "How's your dad?" and you go on walking. And then they shout out an answer and you go on shouting for quite a long distance, because the sound carries.

A SPECIAL
COLOURED BOY

n Sibasa, in those early days when I was working in the local schools, I came across a Coloured [mixed race] boy who showed great potential. There were few Coloured families living in Venda — three or four at most. They came there many many years ago and stayed. Some of the men married Venda women. I told Cecil about this boy and asked if we could advance his education, which we did. During the years of his schooling in Sibasa he would come to show us his work, and we became very close to him. It was a pleasure to watch him grow. Then he went away to school, eventually attending a black university down in the Cape Province and graduating as a teacher. He came home and married a lovely Venda girl, but as time went by, he couldn't handle the political constraints on his life and said he would have to leave and go live somewhere else, where he was free. He was too advanced to remain. I understood this, but of course it was very sad for us all to lose him.

This bright young man went north in Africa proper, where he was interviewed and accepted for a teaching post at a large school. The time came for him to leave, to fly north to his new life and to establish a place to live for himself and his wife, who was now pregnant. The day he flew out, we all went to the airport together. We went up the steps for us; they went up the steps for non-whites, and we stood holding hands across the barrier. As he was about to enter the plane, I saw something for the first time: He held up his right arm and clenched his fist in the Black Power salute. This was his goodbye to South Africa. He was met at the other airport and, on the way to the school, was killed in a car accident.

I lived with guilt for years. We never saw his family again —

they must have hated me for interfering. And I couldn't come to terms with the loss of such a special person.

Years go by and now my son is teaching in a Coloured school. A child approaches him and asks, "Are you the Grahams from Venda, sir? " and "Can I go home and meet your mother? " Can you imagine the joy when we met! This was the baby from the pregnant young woman who had lost her husband in the car crash. She had seen what education had done for him and was determined to make it happen for her son. She was working and providing to send him down here to Johannesburg, to boarding school, to get him the best education available. My interference had not helped the father much, but here was the result in this child. It was a chance in a million that my son would teach this boy and so the knowledge be given to me of the child's advancement. I feel much better, now, about the whole affair, and I do sincerely hope that his family are happier, also. Now he, too, is a teacher and he is going back to Venda. It is different, now; there is freedom and life is good, so he is happy. Perhaps the father had to die for the power to be put into the son.

THE TSHIKONA
FLUTES

Just as Professor Isaac Schapera had landed at Mother's front door in Mochudi years before, so a Professor John Blacking, a famous musicologist/anthropologist arrived in our store in Sibasa, Venda, and asked Cecil where he could find a place to stay and study, for a time. "Oh, " said Cecil, "this all sounds very familiar. Go down that path to the house. There sits my wife; if she likes you, you're in. " He came to the house and asked, "Mrs Graham? " and I immediately replied, "Oh my goodness, an English voice! Who are you? " "I'm from Cambridge University and I wish to come and study Venda music here." He was, at the time, at Wits University, in Johannesburg, and wanted to study all the Venda music, from that of the children right through all the ceremonials. I said, "You're on; you can come and live here. "

What a pleasure he was — he stayed two years and was a great influence in my life, awakening all my anthropological instincts. I watched everything he did, read all his papers, listened to the stories of his trips to the interior. It was heaven for me. I had been studying some of the same things, but here was a professional I could watch at his work.

I loved the Venda music right from the beginning, and I started collecting all the instruments — all the stringed ones, the flutes, all the drums, the calabash rattles, the seed rattles, the hand pianos (*mbilas*), and the large floor *mbila* played by two men. I got all the Venda instruments for men, women, boys, and girls and started studying them, having discovered that I was living amongst one of the most musical tribes in South Africa.

Because they lived in the tropics, there were many natural resources for making instruments: reeds, gourds, wild sisal for strings, large trees for the drums, cattle for the skins, bamboo, and other trees for key instruments. It was all there. The further south you go in South Africa the greater the difficulty in finding the correct materials to create instruments, and as all musicians make their own instruments, the people of Venda had a distinct advantage. (Remember, this is the southern hemisphere, so going south is moving away from the tropics.)

It was inevitable that music would become a large part of my black life. It meant a great deal to me. I loved the music, the people who played it, the ceremonies, and the parts I played when allowed to dance and belong.

The *lugube* is the stringed instrument for married women, and so for me. You place the end of a bamboo reed in your mouth so that the inner mouth becomes the sound box. A string is attached to the bamboo from top to bottom, and you place a finger on it to make the length of string identify the note. As you pluck the string, moving the first finger up and down the string, you change the note. It is simple music, personal music, played by the woman for herself and for her own enjoyment. Many instruments and a lot of music is for private enjoyment, with a few simple notes. The great music is for the tribe or community, when everyone takes part in groups. Just as there is a special song the women sing when they pound the mealies, so each chief will have a special man to play a horn (*phala phala*). This will be the horn of the huge buck called a kudu, or that of a smaller antelope, and it is blown whenever the chief walks anywhere or wishes to announce something, as well as at the beginning of every great ceremony. The horn player does have other tasks in life, but this function — when he blows the horn — is similar to that of the mace carrier in front of a monarch. It is a special honour.

This involvement with music gained me great acceptance with the Venda, and they welcomed me everywhere. When Cecil was away on business trips, sometimes, and I didn't have to worry about his dinner, etc., then, if a ceremony was interesting, I wouldn't go back home. I remember one night coming back in the middle of the night and my neighbour came out and said, "Good heavens, Rae, where have you been? We've been worried! I nearly went to the police!" I said, "It's OK; calm down, I'm fine." "But you've been out all night — with *them!* " "Well, " I said, "here I am to show you that nothing is wrong; I'm fine."

" Whites found it difficult to accept that what I was doing was quite safe, that I was out with my friends and that nothing, but nothing, would ever happen to me. No other whites — men or women — were ever interested in joining me, nor did they ask me any questions. But I was interested in the culture and in being a part of it.

The roads were bad and communications were poor, so I would pack up food and water for Professor Blacking and off he would go to see ceremonies and functions in remote places in the bush. On his return I was bursting with questions. Once, when I asked what he had learnt, he said, "the whole concept of the flutes. "

In Venda we have a special valley called *Tshaulu*, where there is a grove — the only place — where the bamboo called *musununu* grows. It must have come in long ago in the entrails of a bird, a seedeater who carried it and deposited it there. Because it is unique, it is special.

The village is ruled by a queen, instead of the normal chief, which is highly unusual. That came about a long time ago when the Vendas were having one of their battles against the Shangaans, a nearby tribe whom they fought regularly. The Venda were losing the battle and retreated up a little hill. As they did so, the Venda women — who saw their menfolk were losing — picked up stones and rocks and threw them down on the Shangaans. The baboons on the hillside got a fright, and it is said that they, too, joined in and threw stones. The Shangaans then became frightened and fled. From that time on, a woman has always ruled in that area, as thanks to the women who saved the day.

The queen in charge of this place is called Madadzhi. (People often say, "Oh yes, I've heard of her — the Rain Queen." But no, the Rain Queen is not my tribe at all; she is a Lobedu called Mudjadji and lives near Pietersburg. She is still alive, the title is inherited, and the daughter is always in training. This practise has been going on for generations. There has always been a Rain Queen.)

My queen's role in life is one related to a most important musical instrument, the reed flutes called the *Tshikona* flutes, played only by men. The bamboo grows in sections, so you start off with small-length, high-pitch flutes and progress longer and longer to the bass voice flute, covering two or three segments of bamboo.

A set of flutes is in sevens, because the Venda scale is seven. You can have many flutes, but they always go up in groups of seven, according to how many men are present. Each male learns one flute only (one note) and its position in the pattern of the music played. As young boys, they commence learning on a simple flute from river reed — not the same bamboo but a flute nonetheless. The boys will master music at a simple level, then move ultimately to the more advanced music on the *musununu* flutes.

Playing the *tshikona* flutes is complicated: The men dance in a circle as they play, and their feet must be in tune to a full set of five drums, which have a beat of their own. It's like dancing a polka with your feet whilst you hum a waltz — very difficult, and it takes a lot of practise. People who hear the music for the first time think it's a simple form of folk music, but that's because their ears are not adjusted to the different scale and halftones and they do not realise the difficulties involved.

There are set roles in music, in Venda: some is played by boys, some by girls, some by women, others by men. And each group has its own specific instruments. There are also set patterns of procedure.

One man, the leader, has the note which starts each piece of music. He is an important person in the Venda society, and his role has to be earned. His lead flute will have a carved design on it along with his name, to identify it and emphasise its importance. This man will be known not only in his immediate area but by others as well. When large gatherings take place and there are many groups playing, all the lead flute players will be recognised and probably known by name. The leader's flute note is always the same, throughout Venda, but this form of music is not played with the other nine black South African tribes.

The flutes are like an organ of men, with each pipe blown in its proper sequence. There is no limit to what can be played on these very simple flutes.

Tshikona is also the name of our national anthem. Most overseas people regard our great instrument as the drums of Africa, but the flutes have probably a more important role in Venda, as the national anthem cannot be played without them. *Tshikona* is played every day on the radio to start the day and every Venda who can will certainly listen in, to return to his heritage, to have his national anthem in his soul. The soul of the music and the country is in *Tshikona*.

The full name of the national anthem is *Lwa ha masia khale e tshivhila,* which means "The time you run off and leave the pots to boil over" — literally, that when you hear this music you leave everything and run to follow it. This music always puts a special stamp on any occasion.

Once in the history of Venda — and once only — the *tshikona* flutes were played by young girls. A certain chief wanted his crowning ceremony to be different and long remembered, so he instructed that a team of girls be taught the flute music and be allowed to play on the great day. It was a great success, and it certainly has been long remembered. The dance took the form of a blessing. At every great function there is a blessing and a special praise song. The praise song would have been written specially for the chief and remains his praise song for life. It is always sung for him wherever he goes.

Recently, the King of Zululand came to Johannesburg, where he visited the Council Chambers and had dinner with the Mayor. When His Majesty arrived, he had with him a full entourage of headmen and a man in front who sang the king's praises for a half-hour. He is a very important king, so obviously his praise song must be very long. The praise songs are like poems, written about the chief or king, his background, his good future, and so on. Wherever he goes, his praise song and his national anthem will be played. The praise song is a personal song; when the king dies, it is sung for the last time. (When a chief is coming, it is not necessary to learn the song in advance of his arrival; he always has his own praise song singer, who goes everywhere with him. No one else sings the song.)

TSHIKOMBELA

After good rains, in Venda, I noticed there was a teenage girls' ceremony called *Tshikombela,* which is quite special and has a very definite dress. The girls must have passed puberty, so they are young, very strong, and able. I once saw a photograph of them dancing, in the window of a travel bureau in America, and it said, "Come to Africa and see this dance of the young men. " They are not men, of course, but young girls. They wear skirts and a colourful bath towel wrapped round the waist, white shirts, black waistcoats, and trilby hats, so I suppose they do look a bit like men — particularly since they have short, tight hair. But this dance is only for young girls. They wear lots of beads and belts round the waist, rattles on their legs, and chiffon handkerchiefs tied round the upper arm.

Tshikombela has a role to play in spreading news and goodwill from area to area. The girls of a certain village will prepare their music and dance and then walk out on a visit to other villages, near and far. Whilst they stay they are fed and looked after, and in return they will perform. Some of the songs will have stories to tell and messages to give, so they act as did the early itinerant musicians of medieval Europe, who went round with a lute, stopping in castles, singing and disseminating news.

These girls are literally locking together the districts and keeping alive their traditions. There are twelve royal families in Venda, and each one will send out its team to tour and visit and sing songs of their deeds. Each royal family has a chief with full rights; he owns the territory. The members of the tribe are not blood relatives, but different groups who came together centuries ago. The Venda are not a pure tribe, therefore, but a composite one. Each of the chiefs has great power in his region, over which he, alone, exerts control. Land allocation, disputes, ownership questions all come under him. The Paramount Chief is the main one who represents Venda. (The Zulus and the Xhosa each have but one royal family.)

When I first arrived in 1948, before independence, the Paramount Chief would hold meetings and all the chiefs would go to his place for talks on general policy. Each of the others would have his full say. Now, with a Cabinet — since independence — it is different; some of the chiefs were successful in becoming part of the new government, but not all of them.

TRIBAL SCHOOLS

n spite of new programs and educational systems, there remain the traditional "tribal schools " for girls and for boys. A special school will be held for royals — the young of the headmen and chiefs. These "tribal schools " do not function all the time, but are called by chiefs when there are sufficient youngsters to make it run successfully. The boys attend for three months, in which time they are taught how to become men. They kneel naked in ice cold streams without complaining; they fight fierce stickfights to develop their strength. They also have to endure circumcision without an anaesthetic. Only six to ten young men participate at a time, and they are treated very much as *prima donnas* and given lots of attention. As the group is small, they live in one hut with their teacher for the whole three months.

When they graduate there is a beautiful party where they are dressed in special clothing — woven grass skirts and bands across the chest, and a reed mask over the face with bird feathers on top. These costumes are really quite spectacular. The grass of the skirts is woven in wide bands and wound round and round the body until a skirt is created, rather like a kilt. The headdress of reeds looks like a knight's helmet, completely covering the face and giving anonymity. The head of this helmet sprouts the bird feathers. It is very glamourous and strange to see these young men dancing in the wild bush, far from anywhere, so dressed. When they dance you cannot recognize them at all. Their voices, too, are concealed, as they have a bone whistle in their mouth and talk and sing through the sound of the whistle.

When they perform their graduation dance, they wear this

costume barefoot, sometimes with ochre painted on the legs; their arms are painted white. The drums play and they dance to the whole community to show they are no longer boys, but men, with a more fulfilling place in society. In the dance, they come out of the huts one at a time and perform solo, with the parents and local people sitting round watching and trying to guess who it is. They dance to a full set of five drums and are quite athletic, almost balletic, as they perform their jumps and twirls. After this, they will be accepted in the tribe as men.

The girls go to school for nine months — the life cycle of the baby in the womb — as the cycle from girlhood to womanhood. Girls, too, are circumcised, to make the delivery of babies easier. In the Vusa school, as in the others, the royals learn their tribal history and music in addition to taking part in the circumcision ceremonies.

As the weak, in black societies, die, and only the strong propagate, the children who do make it are physically fit. This is important particularly for the young girls, who must be able to do the heavy work required of them in later life — the building of huts, brickmaking, ploughing of fields, etc.

At the school, the girls will become good drummers, learn all about sex — how babies are made, how they are born, and how to keep their husbands happy — as well as their legends and dances. The teaching, for a great part, is done through songs, with the girls singing back the answers. Phrases of knowledge are sung and danced to over and over — a very pleasant way of learning and one which works very well. The teachers are not young but middle-aged and old. The master of the school is an old man, who looks after all these beautiful young girls. When the girls enter the school, all their hair is shaved off, and as it grows it is cut into a small cap. You can tell how much of the nine months has passed by the length of their hair. By the end of the nine months' school the hair cap is quite thick, and they place feathers in their hair from birds trapped for them by the boys, who make sticky traps with natural gum from the trees.

You don't often see the "tribal school" girls walking round the countryside, but whenever I heard there was a school going in a certain area, I would go to visit. It was all right because I'm a woman. When the girls dance, they wear no clothes except for a small loincloth of striped material called *salempore,* with a small strip hanging down over their buttocks on which are sewn a lot of small metal bells and beads. They wear metal bracelets on their arms and legs. I have danced their dances with them many times. They allowed me to do it with my clothes on, as I wasn't a virgin and was just joining in.

I have seen from forty to 250 girls in a school at a time. The local headman will be the one to decide if there are a sufficient number in his area to call a school. There have to be enough girls past puberty, but it doesn't matter if you have to wait a year or two, so the ages within a group will vary from thirteen to seventeen. They will go with gifts and pots of beer, and they pay cash for the school fees. They pay the headman because during the nine months they have to be fed, special huts are built for them to live in, and they belong to that man for the whole time. They never go home. If a project must be done in the headman's village he uses them as a work force. They will build roads, bridges or causeways across a river, they will plough his lands, or build whatever large scale development he requires. The most physically strong in any tribe are the young teenage girls. They are the ones who not only will have the babies, which they carry on their backs as they work, they will walk miles carrying wood on their heads for the fire and water in pots from the river and do any other heavy manual labour.

The headman will look at his territory and look at its local community needs and then see if he has enough girls for a school. It will also depend on how long ago he had such a school. The girls will benefit, he will benefit, and the community will benefit. All this goes into his decision. You will see them all working together, singing and laughing, with the lesson times in between. They are growing into strong, healthy women, ready for life in every way. It is a happy, bonding time, as they make lifelong friendships and learn all the traditional things. It is exciting to them, and when they finish they graduate with a special ceremony called *Domba. Domba* is actually the name of a dance, where they form two long lines, weaving round in circles, the leaders coming together, passing, and going round again. I have danced this dance too — mostly in the line, but once I was allowed to be the leader, right at the front of all the girls locked onto me, rather like a snake.

I will never forget that ceremony. It took place near my home with my immediate chief, Mphaphuli. I was only about thirty years old. Mphaphuli was youngish when I first arrived, which was great for me, as I got to know him very well. I used to walk down the red path through the lands, down to his place of many huts, where his dear old mother and I became friends. He got married in the Christian way. I knew him for ten years; then he was killed in a car accident, and a headman took charge until the chief's son was old enough to rule.

This system of chiefs is quite similar to early Scottish history, with clans and lords in each area and a king or queen over them all. The Zulu structure is also quite similar. There is a well-known Zulu, Welcome Mmsomi, who was the first to translate Shakespeare into Zulu. He chose Macbeth as his first play. It is called *Mmabatho* in Zulu, and of course the whole play, with its fighting and vying for power, the ruthless killing and supplanting of one ruler for another, makes good Zulu sense. Welcome said, "It's easy for us to act this play; it is so similar to our own history. " The *Domba* ceremony, the coming-of-age party, is when the girls are sold, and at this function the whole village will come to participate: The men are looking to see if there is anyone they wish to purchase. In Venda, even a relatively poor man will have two wives. Many men have several. This system may seem strange to us, but I have black women friends who prefer their life to mine. One, who is the fourth wife of a prince, told me she has plenty of freedom to study and to go to university Monday through Friday, knowing her children are happily looked after by the other wives (often regarded as mothers by the children. You often will hear blacks talk about their two or three mothers.) She is with her husband on weekends and so is able to live two lives extremely well.

The headman in Venda would visit a family and arrange a marriage with the parents, establish a bride price, then go back to the other family with the deal. A headman is not a chief, but he is a very important man in the community. Once a deal is struck, a man can commence paying the girl's parents. He doesn't get his bride until the final payment is made.

I once had a Venda gardener in Johannesburg who wanted a certain girl, very well connected with some royal blood, so she was quite expensive. He went off home to do the negotiations with his headman and paid the headman the first down payment. This went on for many months. He was crazy to have set his sights so high, because she was too expensive and she would have wanted a hut with everything in it, and the gifts to her family would have to be large. He was hitching himself to a large financial commitment. Long before he finished making the payments, one of the mine workers, going home with big money, bought her for cash. Fortunately, there is some justice in this system: His headman said to my gardener, "You have paid so much, this amount will now be retrieved from that family, and I will put it down on another girl." I was delighted, because he found someone much cheaper, with much greater compatibility, and she would give him care and love and not be difficult. It all worked out well. He accepted the situation and, once he went home again, he set up his new home and met his new wife, and everything came together because that was a fully acceptable pattern of behaviour. I went to the wedding of the chief's son, once — a very high class wedding, in Venda. It took place in the huts, but it was a very big wedding. He had chosen a well-connected royal girl, so all was well, until the wedding day. There were all the people, the music, the drums of homemade beer, the noise and happy excitement. The bride was brought out by her women, and the chief's son immediately saw that she was pregnant. He knew it wasn't his, and he said, "Oh no, no, no. I'm not going to marry you. " The wedding was all arranged, everything laid on, and there I was with my wedding present, sitting and waiting, and now there was no bride. I was wondering what on earth would happen. I was the only white there, among hundreds and hundreds of people. When the bridegroom said he would not marry her, the headman took her away. The bridegroom walked round the crowd, saw a pretty girl, and said, "You will do," and brought her out into the open place and married her — just like that. She must have been delighted, because she had done very well indeed by marrying a chief's son and making a good future. It wasn't the end of the world for him, as he would have many other wives and this one would be so grateful and would love him dearly.

I should mention that when I attend these functions among my black friends, I am careful always to observe their traditions and sit only with the other, older married women — the mothers — as is proper.

THE DAY THE
BRIDE SMILED

One day I heard the drums playing and followed the sound to see what was happening. It was a Christian wedding, but done with lots of traditional window dressing. A combination of my two worlds. This was about 1955.

The wedding took place in a sort of communal courtyard formed by a circle of thatched huts. Tables were set up between the huts, and everything took place out in the open, under a hot, sunny sky. Though I arrived without asking, I knew it would be fine; I was always welcomed. I asked where to sit and was placed with my age group, the older married women. I knew, as I joined my group of women, that in time our turn would come to dance. Each group takes part in the celebration and becomes really involved.

Trestle tables were covered with white tablecloths, copied from the white culture, but there were three large wedding cakes and they were pink, lemon, and green. On one side was a forty-four gallon drum of homemade beer, made from white mealies boiled over a fire, fermented with yeast, and then strained — slightly bitter but very nutritious, and a common drink in Venda.

When the bride arrived she was dressed in a large white sort of crinoline dress, very elaborate. She had many bridesmaids, as every cousin and relative wanted to be involved and it didn't cost much because each girl made her own dress. They all arrived in a long procession and sat down along the tables.

A black wedding has lots of speeches. No one is inhibited, and all the important people will expect to be asked to speak. It is a joyful occasion — the joining not just of two families but of two communities. You don't have to invite black people to a wedding; they just arrive.

They all belong and they all take part.

A certain part of a tribal wedding is that the bride must not smile or look happy. She is leaving home and must look sad about that. All day long on the wedding day she must look sad. (Although she is having a Christian wedding and is dressed in a Christian wedding dress, she still must perform tribally. Just as she will have been paid for tribally, with the brideprice called *lobola*.) She is leaving home to go live with another group of people, and there is a prescribed pattern of behaviour.

The time came for my group to dance. We formed a long line right in the middle of the ceremony, in front of the bride and groom. The drums were playing and we bent over and pranced and performed with vigour. It was such fun, and I always laugh a lot when I'm having a good time, and I made some mistakes in the dance and THE BRIDE SMILED. She didn't burst out laughing, but she smiled. It was a distinct break in tradition and forever after, that wedding was called by the people, "The Day the Bride Smiled."

TOP: *The Standard Bank, Ltd. "branch office" in Mochudi (a concrete slab with some wood posts for the sign!)* BOTTOM: *Typical Botswana scene, in good times.*

FACING PAGE, TOP: *Bakagalahadi School, with a cardboard "blackboard."* FACING PAGE, BOTTOM: *A typical camp of Rae Graham's with canvas folding beds; Bakwena people are coming for a visit.*

TOP: *A Bakwena house,*
Botswana; Chaena in the
middle was often Rae's
helper-tracker. BELOW:
Women pounding mealies
in a Bakwena village.

FACING PAGE, TOP:
Bushwomen gathering food
in the Kalahari Desert. The
last woman in the group
carries her baby on her
back. FACING PAGE, BELOW:
A Bushman house.

Top: *Food gathering in the Kalahari Desert.* Bottom: *Cecil Graham with a Bushman.* FACING PAGE, top: *A Bushman's hunter's kit.* FACING PAGE, bottom: *Bushman divining bones.*

TOP: *Bushman grand-
mother and two
granddaughters,
Kalahari Desert.*
BOTTOM: *Colette, left,
and Felicity Graham
with a Bushman
hunter.* FACING PAGE,
TOP: *Drawing in the
Kalahari Desert.*
FACING PAGE, BOTTOM:
*Mashudu reading the
bones for a villager,
edge of the Kalahari,
Botswana.*

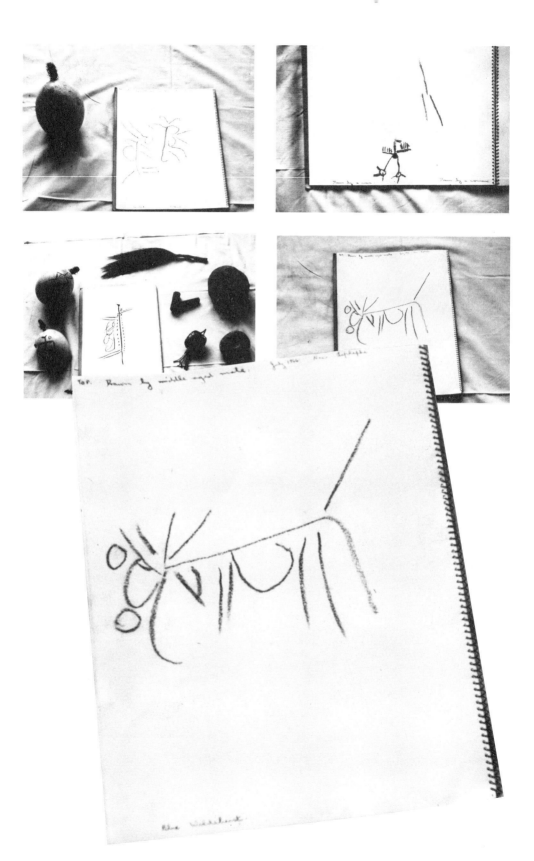

FACING PAGE: *Bushman drawings, clockwise from upper left: 1. A buck lying down, as he would be seen when killed by the hunter. 2. Two ostriches, a symbolic one drawn by a woman and a more literal one drawn by a male hunter. 3. A wildebeest (also shown larger) with eyes drawn outside the body because of the way they show up at night. 4. A gemsbok with long horns.*
THIS PAGE: *Rae Graham (Mashudu) and Bushmen at drawing sessions.*

MOCHUDI, BOTSWANA

My first introduction to Mochudi was shattering. This was in 1948, when we spent a few days there before going to live in Venda. There was so little to do. Not even Saturday tennis, as in Sibasa. The second year was better, because I had my baby boy and something to do. I remember going off walking with him up to the well, just to see the people.

The journey down to Mochudi had taken us a whole long day, because not only was it far but it is cattle country and we were motoring through farms, and across the road every now and then were large metal gates that had to be opened and then shut again. Local children would wait on the roadside, open the gate for us to drive through, and wait for a handful of sweets. We never travelled anywhere without a large bag of sweets to give away. The last stop was Mafeking, where I bought carrots, potatoes, and lettuce. When we got to Mochudi, I would bury the root vegetables in the garden in the sand, because they dried out and kept quite well in the ground, for whenever I needed fresh vegetables for my baby. I remember one day when a black friend arrived to visit and saw me on my knees, sifting carefully through the sand. "What are you doing? " she asked. I was near to tears and said, "My son is sick and I want to make him some good food, and I can't find a single carrot. " But it was of no use; there wasn't one, and there was nowhere to get one, either.

In my kitchen, now, you will find some coal on the table. When you have tired vegetables, dried out and miserable looking, place them in cold water with a few pieces of coal and they will soak in the carbon and freshen up. Any housewife who lives in desert country will tell you that tip. Whenever I went down there from Johannesburg, I didn't take boxes of chocolates for presents, but salads and green things, and no matter how they arrived they could be freshened with coal. I always spent May in Mochudi, for stocktaking, and then later in the year when our store manager, Johnny, and his wife, Elsa, went away on holiday to escape the heat. I was there for Christmas, once. Even in the southern hemisphere, it was the hottest Christmas in my life. I had two children to make a party for, but I didn't do a roast turkey; it was just too hot for any roast dinner.

I also remember discovering the very large black king ants. If you trod on one of them your shoes would smell of rotten bad eggs, so bad that you couldn't wear those shoes for a few days, so you always looked out for those ants as you walked.

I learnt very quickly that Botswana was primarily cattle country and relied on the sale of meat and skins for its economy. All over the country, wells were put down a cow's day's march apart, because if you can walk and water cattle, then you can move anything. We had our own borehole, next to the house. Johnny made a machine out of the engine from an old motor-bike and that would pump every day for an hour or so, just enough for us, our staff, and workers. Then it was left to recover until the morrow. One was judicious in those days; no waste of precious resources.

When Professor Schapera chose to come and live with Mother and Father for a few years, to study the Bakghatla people, it was because they, of all the different groups, had a unique and perfect African village and tribal system — one that worked and was worth recording for posterity. He saw the great value of this place. Now, with the introduction of Western materials and standards, the village has changed completely, so much so that recently we were approached by the Bakghatla educational authorities in Mochudi, with a plea for any material we might have from those early years: They want to make a museum, to show what their people were all about. Chief Isang Pilane knew exactly what should be done but, alas, his ideals are no longer respected.

I started going out into the huts, to see if these people were different to the Venda, and of course they were. They don't live in family units on their lands as the Venda did. The Bakghatla live in communities, large villages up to 6000 people — a real township with foot paths and roads (sand, but nevertheless roads), and a central chief's place with a *kgotla* (meeting house). The grazing lands are all together, far out. In the evening I could see the blue smoke of cooking fires — the blue smoke of Africa — because in Botswana there is plenty of dry wood lying everywhere and you don't have to look far for fuel. You must know what to collect, however, as there are certain trees that have poisonous sap and if you make a fire with them and cook meat over the smoke you will die. You must know which are the hard woods that make charcoal fire, which are the soft woods that burn well just for light. You must know which trees you never camp and sleep under, because they have loose bark behind which certain insects live that would bite you. Lots of interesting bits of information I accumulated slowly. Veldtlore.

One of the old men, an Afrikaner called Meneer [Mr] Knobel, knew all the plants in the veldt and became famous for discovering a new, unlisted one of the *stapelia* family. It was then named after him — *Knobelia Stabilis,* a cactus plant. He would take me out walking, showing me this plant, that geological set of rocks, the other tree and so on, and I watched and listened keenly, trying to identify things as we walked. It is all sand, there, and I would try to observe our position in relation to the small hill in the village. After some time, Mnr Knobel would say, "Fine, now you take us home, " and of course it was the old story — you walk in circles. I'm not stupid, and I knew a bit of the bush by this time, but I could never get us back. The sun had moved too much, certain trees just kept coming up, and I knew that I was lost.

"You see," said my teacher then, "people say there is nothing out here in the semi-desert, but it is full of things if you learn how to look. There are scores of varieties of wild grass, insects of many kinds. " Later, I would take my family on holidays into the bush, always with a project of some sort to help us learn. On one trip we found twenty different kinds of praying mantis. On another trip, with my black friend Mothlohelwa (whose name means "the one who is left behind," as he was born of elderly parents who knew he would grow up without them), we learnt that wild animals don't usually attack something that is quite still. At a cheetah sanctuary, one day, a cheetah was between my youngest daughter, Natalie, and me. She froze quite still and the cheetah took a leap over her and was gone! The secret is not to react with noise and aggression but quietly to talk, and create assurance. The same with snakes — even cobras.

The people of Botswana lived with much hardship, due to long droughts. I was there through two of them. I remember that I would drive through the village and on my way see a cow standing still under a tree, but on my return it would be dead. All the women could do was use the meat and cure the skin, but they had lost the cow as a milk source and as breeding stock, and cattle were their life blood. It was desperately hard.

Overseas, the United Nations decided to send in relief, to send food, but they did it without asking anyone, not even us locals, and so they sent the wrong things. They sent in masses of American cornmeal, which is bright yellow, but the blacks wouldn't eat that meal at all: *Our mealies are white white.* The women were told to go to the local schools and they would be given food. They queued up in long lines and after some wait received their portion of the meal, only to be bitterly disappointed. They went round the school building and threw it away, because it was a foreign meal unknown to them and they wouldn't eat it. How frustrated I was with that waste of money, all sent with the best of intentions. (Nowadays, imported yellow meal is mixed with our own white meal and so is acceptable.) I knew that what was really needed was cattle food, to keep the economy alive and ensure the future, but no one ever thought of that, and none came, and the cattle died in thousands. The sands were covered with drying skins ready for market, which provided money for the short term, so people lived, but their future was bleak. There were always some veldt foods such as wild melons, wild cucumbers, *tsamma* melons, and beans that grew underground in pods, but the real need was never addressed. Later on, the need was fertiliser for the dry lands, but that also never came.

In those days I didn't know anyone in authority to whom I could explain my anguish. It taught me a great lesson about what to do and what not to do, in Africa — a continent of continual problems with mistakes made easily because of lack of communication. It reminds me of an experience in Johannesburg when a friend and I used to take our two families into the Coloured township on Christmas day, to a large home for orphans. We would tell the staff to go home and spend Christmas with their own families and we moved in and made the dinner and a party for the whole group of Coloured children — at least 100 of them. Our two husbands and all our children worked like Trojans. It was our way of making Christmas truly Christian. Many people gave us food, gifts, etc., and one wealthy lady insisted on giving us strawberries — fresh ones — for the whole 100 children. I said to her, "Please, please, rather give us the money for more meat." "Oh, no," she said, "they must have a real treat." Of course the inevitable happened: The children didn't eat the strawberries. They had never seen any and after one bite didn't like them. All that fruit went into the dustbin, and I cried inside, thinking of what I could have done with all that money.

Botswana has a culture very close to Nature. The manna corn is not grown round their huts, as in Venda. Rather, the whole village is developed as a rural townplace and the lands are far out, a wagon-ride away, where everyone has a plot of land — quite large. Out there are more huts — not as well constructed as the village homes, but places to live in when it is ploughing time or planting time. Then the village is empty, except for the old women and small children, as everyone moves out to the lands. It is most festive. The ploughing is done with cattle pulling a plough blade, guided by a man walking behind. It is hard work because the land has been baked hard by the sun.

Once the corn is growing and the small plants are breaking through, the young children of the village sleep in little lean-to's on the lands, to keep the birds away from the seed. In this season, my father-in-law would pack up all the necessary items and move out to our subsidiary store, so that the people could get all their requirements without the long trek back to the village. We had a large three-ton truck, so stocks could regularly go out to that store. Very little business was taking place in the village. We would move the staff, as well, and we would have a real veldt life — my children would run free, right out there in the wilds. It was beautiful, and I never tired of the tranquility, the rightness of it all: this pattern which had existed for so long, and the noises of the people round their fires in the evenings, the cattle bells ringing as they came into the *kraal* for the night. (Each lead cow wears a metal bell round its neck.) It was a joyous time of year when we packed up and went out in long lines, all the wagons drawn by oxen, the people sitting on top of their goods, laughing and talking, accepting the hard work and looking forward to a harvest.

I would take my children onto the lands and let them see and be part of the ploughing — watching the great metal ploughshare cutting into the ground, the sweat of the man and beast, the lovely sound of the cracking whip. This special whip is made of cattle skin called *reims*. It does not *touch* the ox; it is cracked alongside the animals. The *reim* is very long — up to twelve feet — and it is quite an art to crack it just where you want it — alongside the lead ox's head, to encourage him to pull harder. For ploughing there is only one ox, but for pulling the wagons there are many, in pairs, with wooden yokes across each pair. Each one has a name and a different personality.

Those special times live in my memory. When the harvest was collected — if the rains came at the right time and there was a harvest at all — then the wagons would return triumphantly to the village.

TRADING

Mochudi, the village where our Botswana store was located, was a sandy place, with practically no water in the river, ever, but there was a small dam in the middle of the village and a pump over a well, where the women would queue up to fill their pots and buckets. We also had a small borehole of our own.

Chief Isang Pilane, was a great old friend of Father's. He was the last of the really great chiefs. I never knew him; his wife was ruling in 1948 when I first went there, and what a great and clever woman she was.

Isang Pilane was so advanced for his time. He often visited and had supper with Mother and Father and discussed his vision for his people and what he wanted to accomplish for them. The three of them had great companionship and bonding. Colour didn't matter; they were on the same level. In those days, this was was unusual. "I want my people to grow," he would say. "They must learn." He built a school high up on top of a rocky outcrop so the children had to climb quite a steep path of boulders to school, every day, and so keep in good health. He and Father planned and built bridges and roads — Father would use his truck and get the stones and cement, the chief got the labour, and together they made things happen.

The road between Mochudi and the railway line where we would go to fetch goods off the trains was four miles of dreadful, shaking, grinding misery — a very bad road that everyone had to endure. One year, on Father's birthday, he invited all the whites in the village to a picnic *braaivleis* [barbecue] out in the country. There were missionary people, government officials, store people, and borehole people. After good food — Father had killed a sheep, the fires were burning, and everyone was having a happy time — Father announced that it was his birthday. "Oh, no! Why didn't you tell us? We would have given you a present!" everyone said. "Fine;" said Father, "Undo that truck and you will find picks and shovels. You can give me the present of fixing the road!" The entire white community started in to fix it right there and then, and over the next many months each one would provide materials and labour and gradually the road was made. Today, we still call it "Father's Road." It was straightened in many places, but not where one large magnificent wild tree was standing, so there is a big curve.

Fixing this road was great, because that railway halt ("Pilane") was our communication point. The mixed-goods [freight] train came down from Rhodesia, carrying people and goods, and everything we ordered or goods we sent to Johannesburg (skins and hides and bones) were all trucked from there. We also sent live pigs and cattle to market in Johannesburg. It was a very interesting train, so that even if you had nothing arriving on it, it was a nice outing to drive the four miles there and just watch its arrival, to see what was on it.

One day in Father's life, about 1930 — during the Depression — a young man called Johnny Odendaal left his farming home, where there was no food and no money, and went out into the world to find a job. He got onto the mixed-goods train (without a ticket, as he had no money) and jumped off at Pilane and started walking to Mochudi. He arrived and walked into our store and said to Father, "I'm a strong young man. Can I get work, please?" Father told him that times were so hard he was not employing anyone, but that he could work for his food. He did just that and remained with us all his life, working well over forty years as a treasured member of our family. We loved him as an uncle and that is what he became to us and our children — a kind, jolly uncle. He married a nurse who worked in a hospital in Lobatse, some eighty miles away, and she became our Aunt Elsa. They were both Afrikaners, but it didn't matter to us; we loved them.

Johnny used to tell me that he didn't know why he jumped off the train at Pilane, but destiny made him come towards the Grahams and a close life with us. When he left home his father gave him an old army great coat, that's all — no money — and said, "You must go, my boy. We can't feed the whole family, so some must go." Imagine leaving home with nothing and walking across sandy desert to the train, not knowing where next you would sleep or eat. Incredible. When Johnny jumped off the train at Pilane and asked at the railway station what was nearby, they said, "Down that road is a village with two stores — Klaffs' and Grahams — 'but they can't give you work; they are desperate themselves." But he took a chance, and it's very significant that he didn't jump off in a town, but in a desolate siding halt. Very courageous.

One day Johnny got very ill with appendicitis and Father rushed him to the railway line. It was nighttime, but there was a train passing through, so Father lit a big fire on the lines and stopped the train, which took Johnny up to Johannesburg and saved his life.

Johnny taught me lots of important lessons. Outside our store was a fenced-off place with a large pile of bones of all kinds. I was fascinated with the variety, and I was in there, one day, climbing through the pile, examining them, when Uncle Johnny came out of the store, saw me, and yelled, "Get out of there!" I quickly joined him and said, "Oh, I'm so sorry. I didn't know I couldn't do that. What have I done wrong?" He explained, "No matter how old and dry these bones are, lying in the sun, no matter how dry and clean they may look, they still carry anthrax, and if you scrape your skin and it bleeds, it can absorb the anthrax and you die."

The bones were collected all over by the black women and brought to the store, where we weighed them and paid cash for them. When there was a sufficient pile they were trucked off to the railway line and we sent them up to Johannesburg to the glue factory. In those days, glue was not an artificial substance but was created from bones. This was a fantastic way for black women to make money: They just had to roam round the bush and look for dead carcasses. Money for nothing, provided by the Lord, so they could exchange the rubbish in the bush for mealie meal, sugar, etc.

On my first visit to Mochudi I had made a terrible mistake about the bones. I saw all these women with baskets of smelly, dirty bones and said to the storeman, "Tell those women to go away with all that rubbish" and away they went (probably much to the amusement of our staff, who must have thought me quite stupid). The women walked many miles across the village to the other store and sold the bones there. My husband was ill with malaria, at that time, and when I went home at lunchtime he asked, "How are you doing?" It was my first time ever running a store. "Oh super," I said. "I'm running it beautifully. But there were some stupid women with bones." "I hope you took them in and looked after them," he said. "No," I answered, "I sent them away." He then told me what it was all about. I learnt all these things and they became a way of life — so different from England, but I quickly became a part of it all.

Another commodity, there, was the skins. We were very good at skins, and in the early days we made good money with our bones and skins, the way we prepared them. In Venda there was no barter, but in Botswana, yes. Botswana is cattle country, and it used to be that the main economy centred around cattle. (Now the country relies more on its minerals.) A man's wealth was his cattle and his ability to feed them and get them to market in Lobatse, where the canning factory is. This is why the wells — a cow's day's march apart — became so important. This is a very dry country. They do grow a kind of corn — manna — with a small, dark brown kernel that when pounded produces a lovely, thick, brown nutritious porridge, but there is not much mealie meal, as there is often not enough rain. With mealies having to be imported, the value of the trade in skins and bones can be easily appreciated. That is why Cecil's father was so keen to have these extras attached to the business. It was a way of helping to upgrade the people. He was always thinking of ways to do this — such a powerful urge for service.

Outside the storerooms at the back of the store, Father poured cement into big, saucer-like indentations in the sandy floor. These saucers were filled with brine, in which we soaked the skins. The people would bring in the skins roughly cleaned and scraped, dried and sometimes folded so badly they would crack and you couldn't open them flat. This means the quality of the skin is not so good and it brings a low price. The very bad ones were rejected. By soaking the skins in brine, they become soft and pliable and can be stretched out flat and pegged down on the sandy floor. Then, if necessary, they can be rescraped to take off all the fat and bits. In this way, the quality of the rough skin is improved, they can be stacked in large flat piles, roped together and sent off to the train to Johannesburg, where they go to the shoe factories. In this way, Father and Johnny devised a way for the people to get better money for the goat and cattle skins which they did not know how to treat properly themselves.

Those skins really smell in the hot sun, but we became known in Johannesburg for our well-prepared skins and we always got good prices. Leather was a very important commodity and meant good money for Botswana. That and the canned beef. Nobody ever stole the skins, although they just lay out there in the open. As in Venda, society was much more honest, then.

So, Mochudi Trading Store skins were high quality leather. That went for pig skins, too. There were many pigs in the village, along with goats, and sheep of poor quality. Mostly we ate goat. Cows were fine because they could eat the chaff from the manna and could browse in the bush and find enough to eat. Pigs eat all the offal and leftovers from human beings, so nearly every family had a pig. They would bring all these animals to sell to us, so we kept a pen of animals.

The *kraal* where you keep animals is easy to construct: Take a truck out to the bush, cut down thorn bushes (they grow everywhere), place them with the stems inwards and the thick bush of thorns outwards in a circle, keeping a place for the opening where you drive the animals in at night — a separate *kraal* for each kind of animal. Then place another thorn bush into the opening, to close it up. (This for small stock; for cows, a sturdier gate was required — made of dry wood from dead trees.)

Johnny taught us what to do with a pig: You got two men to hold its legs together to make it immobile, then you clenched your fist and thrust it down the throat of the squealing pig. As it retched and opened its throat, you could peer down and see if there were any lumps. It was a method of seeing if the pig had measles, because if it did it was inedible. A lot of the pigs had measles. We bought pigs in large numbers, fattened them up, and then trucked them alive, to Johannesburg. If you didn't know this little trick and trucked up pigs that had measles, you were in trouble. When tested at market and found to have the disease they were shot, and instead of making money you got a bill for their disposal. So we were very fortunate to have learnt this trick and we never sent a sick pig to market. In fact, we never bought a sick one from people who came to sell.

When you truck pigs you must build up the side of the truck so they cannot see the moving road. If they do, they get dizzy and die.

On my first visit to Mochudi I saw and visited Queen Pilane and got to know her quite well. Years later, when I was staying there with three of my children, I went to call on her. I always wore long, cotton wrapover skirts or long, full-length kaftans, in black countries — never trousers. It is not dignified for women to wear trousers, and it is not correct for women to look like men. Short dresses are difficult to handle when you sit on the floor. The long skirts are feminine and dignified and can easily be washed, so there is no problem in sitting on red dirt floors. The two black countries I lived in were like this, even though they were quite different in other respects: Venda — lush, tropical, green, with many flowers, trees, and plants, the red dust and lots of music; and Botswana — sandy, dry desert, very quiet, no drums, very few musical instruments, more introverted people, only scrub, no large trees.

When I first had to live for a long time in Mochudi, I surveyed the territory to see what I could do. You can't walk so far, there, because it is too hot and dry, very debilitating. There was a soccer field next to our house and store, so often there was a game I could go and watch. Lots of people, lots of noise and excitement — great fun. On the other side of the field lived my nearest neighbour, Mrs Fitz, a Coloured lady who ran a small shop selling sweets, lemonade, and her own homemade bread, which she baked in a large ants' nest at the back of her house. Ants' nests are made of clay worked with saliva by the ants, so they are just like a large clay heap. If you dig a hole into it you have a perfect oven. Her bread was famous, and I always watched for when the smoke was curling up, then waited an hour or so and went over to buy fresh, hot, delicious bread. We became good friends and often sat and had chats and tea together. There were not many Coloureds in Mochudi. Her husband and his family were wagon builders and wheel makers — a fairly good way to make a living. Mrs Fitz was the only person in the village who made bread, so she was special. I would take hours to buy a loaf so that I could have her company. She also had the only piano, and what a joy that was! (Up at the top of the village, at the stone mission church, they had a small pump organ. The services were mostly in Tswana and Afrikaans.)

My children got to know and love that piano, and they would go off visiting Mrs Fitz. She knew why they had come, and after a little while she would say, "Go and wash your hands and you may play the piano." This was a great treat. Years later, when they were all grown, one of them asked, "That lady with the piano, she was black, was she?" They didn't remember what she was, because it didn't matter; she was just a friend. I remembered that for a long time.

At the back of our house, Johnny dug holes and put down forty-four gallon drums, filled them with good soil we brought in, and then planted orange and lemon trees for the fruit and the shade. In-between the trees we could plant vegetables and run water. This was after we had a borehole; in the early days, there was not enough water to do all this planting.

We ate a lot of dried beans, peas, maize, rice, lentils, and all the kinds of food that keep in a hot climate with no trouble. We had a butcher shop — a small room on one side of the big store — and twice a week we would kill one animal. Everyone knew which day, and they came down for it, because with no refrigeration nothing could be stored. On one side there was a large concrete slab made under a tree. The animal was tied up on the slab, shot, then skinned and cleaned and thoroughly washed, cut and sawn into reasonable-sized pieces, and carried in large enamel basins to the butcher shop. It was sold at one shilling [14¢] per pound for every part of the beast, whether goat, pig, sheep, or cow. No one seemed to mind about whether they got the best bits or not. I always was allowed to choose what I wanted first, so I often would take the liver and kidneys, the choice fillet, and a large shin bone for making soup. I can cook goat just as tender as sheep; you wouldn't know the difference.

We made biltong [jerky] in our house for ourselves. Blacks are not natural biltong eaters and don't make it. Biltong is made from muscle, specially cut and soaked in herbs, spices, salt, sugar, and vinegar, then hung on a line to dry. It keeps forever, once dry, and is very useful if you have someone sick. You can grate it on bread and butter. I had one baby — my second daughter, Colette — who was allergic to milk. I couldn't breast feed her or give her cow's milk, so I brought her up on powdered biltong in water, which is full of protein. It was because of Colette's illness that we moved from the store in Venda to the one in Botswana: We could get licenses to hunt, in Botswana; in Venda there is no game. Auntie Elsa, Johnny's wife, became like a mother to me and helped to grate the wildebeest [gnu] biltong to feed the baby.

The things we lacked and sometimes craved were fresh green vegetables and salads. Oh, how I longed for a lettuce.

Botswana is now very successful, for several reasons. Sir Seretse Khama went to university at Oxford, married a white English woman and had Coloured children. Because of this, he was able to bridge the cultures. He started a real democratic government and — with investigation by large companies — found minerals that have put the country on a good economic footing. Seretse is now dead, but I knew him well. I met him as a student at Oxford. Cecil had said, "Come and meet someone from home," and it was this royal chief's son! He became the first ever President of Botswana.

Seretse married Ruth in England and came to live in Mochudi. He couldn't go up and live with his tribe, the Bamangwato, because they had difficulty with his white wife. The country wasn't Botswana, yet; it was under British rule and was called the Bechuanaland Protectorate. This was around 1953. The British had to do something with him, so they gave him a small house in our village, with a small income. Their life was pretty dull, without much contact. When he became a political embarrassment he and Ruth were moved to London, where they lived in exile for years, until he came back to a new, free country, Botswana (meaning "place of the Tswana "), and became the President, which role he fulfilled with distinction until his death.

I so well remember the weeklong Independence celebrations, terminating in the parade to the stadium, where the Union Jack came down and the new flag went up, at midnight. H.R.H. Princess Marina came out to represent the Queen. She stood there in a full-length embroidered gown and wearing a tiara, in a full- scale dust storm so bad that visibility was only a few yards.

The trumpets couldn't play because they were full of dust. We were all huddled down, with scarves tied over our mouth and nose, because it was difficult to breathe. But it was an electric, exciting moment. Sir Seretse Khama stood in the middle of the stadium, all alone, all the great lights shining on him. What a moment, when the new flag was raised and the whole stadium cheered and shouted, and then — for the first time — the new national anthem was played. After all those bitter years, Seretse was now their leader, and what a great success he made of it.

Princess Marina was magnificent, although she was not young, then. She stood undaunted, with dust in her eyes and mouth, truly regal. The next day she officially opened the new hospital in the brand new capital, Gaberone. It was called Princess Marina Hospital. I'm sure that when she got back to England she would have remarked to the Queen, "Your Commonwealth is very dusty, in parts, Your Majesty; next time, *you* go "!

But that was years ahead. When Seretse and Ruth came to live in Mochudi they lived in a very small, humble little house, with little money. When one of the window panes broke, she fixed it up with a piece of cardboard.

There were three English women in the village, but we had nothing to do with one another. The senior lady was the wife of the Distict Commissioner and lived at one end of the village, where his office was. We traders were at the other end of the village, and she certainly did not visit with a trader's wife; we were at the bottom of the social ladder. Poor Ruth was an outcast, almost, whom no one visited.

I felt so sorry for Ruth. She had nothing, really. I had a nice house, with all the comforts, but she led a dull, empty life, just waiting and waiting. Then, of course, the years of exile in London, both of them alone, no one apparently caring what became of them. Those early years for them were horrible, but she stuck with him, all credit to her.

FATHER AND SON

Cecil's early life was much intertwined with our life together in the black countries. He got malaria when he was eight years old and had it all his life (there was no cure, then), until he went to the war and lived in trenches in Italy, in ice and snow. That apparently killed the malaria bug, and he came back to Africa healthy. But all his life he was a delicate child and so did not go away early to boarding school, as his brother did. Instead, Cecil had a teacher, Miss von Mollendorf, who came to live at the mission station in Mochudi and taught him until he was twelve years old, when he went to Pretoria Boys High as a boarder. Miss von Mollendorf never left the village, and when her white pupils all had gone (she also taught the missionary's children), she stayed on and became one of the mission workers among the tribe. She taught them many things and also had classes for the women — sewing, cooking, baby care, first aid, games, and outings. She got me to join with her, and I used to give the First Aid lessons. What good times we had, and what good fellowship and love. She was Auntie Moller to us, and except for the blood, she was a member of the family, like Johnny. The Grahams seem to collect people. We may be short on real relatives, but we have lots of extra people in our lives.

Auntie Moller was a young woman when she came to live and teach in Mochudi, but she was an old lady when finally she retired. When first we arrived back, in October 1948, can you imagine her joy to see Cecil, her little schoolboy, with his M.A. degree from Oxford University? Her foundation teaching had borne great fruit.

On one visit to Mochudi, when our son Clive was one year old, I went off walking in the village — up to the well, where at 5:00 PM the women were fetching water for the evening meal and there were always people to chat to. I had tied the baby on my back, African style. With only one baby it was an easy way to get around — you can't push a pram in sand. I also walked barefoot, as the people did. It was nicer and easier, and what do you want shoes for, in a hot climate? It so seldom rains there. I was busy at the well, making friends and talking to people, saying "*dumela* " ("hello"), when suddenly a woman came rushing up to me, took my baby and began shouting at me. I didn't understand a thing she said and wondered at her excitement. I pointed to where I had come from, at the store, and off she ran with Clive, laughing and talking, with me running after her. She had recognised that this child was the son of the baby she had carried on *her* back: Her name was Orica; she had been Cecil's nanny, and I wish you could see the joy of their meeting, when she found him. There I was, still running behind, when I saw this tall husband of mine come out of the store and this little Tswana woman rush up to him and hug him, both of them laughing, because — although many years had passed — Cecil immediately recognised her, too. They clasped hands, and she hugged him and Clive. It was beautiful to see. We then sat down, and she kept touching me — to establish a bond — whilst Cecil tried to bring back his Tswana language and asked of her family — who was dead, who was there, all the news. Later, as I got to know more people in the village, I used to ask them to tell me about my husband as a child and they would recount stories of his activities. He was called "Witapie" by his friends, which means "white monkey" because he had white/blond hair and very white pasty skin. Father was called "the father of the white hair" ("Rapudutswana") because he also had white hair, as a young man.

QUEEN ISANG PILANE

Queen Isang Pilane of the Bakgathla tribe in Mochudi was an old lady who became a real friend. Like her deceased husband, she was the real head of her people and equally as strong and advanced as he had been. When he died she took on his role splendidly.

The first time I met her, in November 1948, I had just arrived in South Africa and went down to Botswana to visit and just meet her. Some years later, when I was there with my first three children, I went to call and pay my respects. I got dressed correctly, myself, in a dress, but I did a silly thing for the three little ones who were constantly crawling and playing on the sand. Because of their activity, I dressed them in cotton trousers and shirts — all three of them. It was the simplest way to keep the sand out of their nappies [diapers]. I arrived at Her Majesty's place — a circle of huts, some very large, with a large, clean courtyard made of cattle dung. The dung is smoothed and worked in lovely, fanlike patterns made with the fingers as the porridge-like mixture of sand, cow dung and water is smoothed out. When dry, cattle dung floors are perfect in that climate. There is no smell, and with practically no rain it bakes hard. It is swept every day with grass brushes, and it is so clean you can prepare food on it.

The Queen had a lot of handmaidens, and as I approached the opening they came forward and greeted me. "*Dumela*" ("Good day"). "*Dumela*," I said. "Lekae" ("Are you well?") "Riteng" ("We are fine"), they replied. Then they told me Her Majesty would be coming. All round the courtyard are places to sit, incorporated in the walls, all made of clay and cow dung. Simple, beautiful, functional, and very comfortable. I sat on one near the entrance. Across the open space was a throne-like place, also made in the same way, where she could hold audience. Eventually she came, with more women around her, and she sat down. I had leaped to my feet and only sat when she did. She greeted me and then said, "And who are all these little men? "

I got the message immediately. She knew I had only one son. I grabbed them up, apologised, "I'm sorry, Your Majesty. May I visit you another day? " and left. I never made that mistake again. Even as small children, boys wear boys' clothes and girls wear girls' clothes. I had done the unforgivable, dressing two of my daughters in boys' clothing.

On another day, I went back to visit the Queen with my two girls suitably dressed in pretty dresses. She said to me, "I'm so glad you've come back; I have something to show you. " We went outside. Around the huts and some distance away was a very very large granary hut — the kind you build above ground, so the air can circulate underneath. There you can store the grain whilst it is still on the cob. It dries out and will keep a very long time. This is true no matter which grain you have. In Venda it will be mealies on the cob; in Botswana it will be manna. You fill it up to the top, then place branches over it. There it is safe, guaranteeing food for the future.

In Botswana they are famous for their woven mats, baskets, and many products made of grasses, fibres, and reeds. The patterns are quite special, and they can plait and weave incredibly tight, firm baskets that can actually hold liquids — baskets you can carry water in. The Queen's granary was not only sticks but completely covered with woven mats, and it was huge. Every single family coming back from the lands had to bring her a ration of their crops to be placed in this large granary. It was so big you could have placed two motorcars in there, in the corn, without even seeing them.

"Your Majesty," I said, "what a food stock! For how long would it feed people?" "Now, do you want to know why I have done this?" she asked. "When the next drought comes, every family will come, with the same basket they brought it in, and I will give them back their grain. They do not think long-term, so that is how I will give them back food to keep them alive in the bad times." I said, "You know, Your

Majesty, you are a genius," and she was. She had set out a system which was brilliant. She had a padlock on the granary, and she kept the key. No one could get at it until she decided it was time.

You may wonder why the grain had to be locked up, in Botswana, when in Venda it was not. In Sibasa, we — the Grahams — kept the grain for them, in our pits. They never did it for themselves. Here, I imagine, the temptation must have been great for those people whose own grain was in there. Our grain was not the Vendas' until they paid for it, as we had paid them. Here, there was no payment. Also, the Venda didn't live in villages or have this great community. This queen was in control of 6000 people. She felt she must think for the whole group and accepted responsibility for all of them. She was special, and way ahead in her thinking.

When the Queen died, her funeral was a great event. We were there and took part. I have been to lots of black funerals, but this was the most moving of them all. I saw then just how loved she was.

We all wore black. No matter what it was, it had to be black. I had only a pure wool black winter suit, so I wore that, with high-heeled black shoes and stockings, black gloves and a black hat — on a blazing hot day, walking in the desert sand, with thousands of singing Bakghatlas. We were about ten whites (all the whites in the village).

As we walked everyone picked up a stone, which we carried to the place where all the great royals were buried, with graves all marked with tombstones. The big hole had already been dug and as we arrived, her large coffin (she was a very big woman) was brought along on the open wagon drawn by oxen. We were walking slowly, at the pace of the oxen, and the singing never stopped. It was a very moving experience, and I cried. The singing, the general feeling of mourning for someone so loved, so great, it was a tangible joint emotion of so many people. The love, the respect, the pain — they knew what they had lost.

The coffin was placed in the hole and the elders shoveled some earth in. Many people did that, and finally it was completely stamped down. Then we all filed past and placed our stones on the grave until there was a large stone cairn in the Queen's honour, placed there by the people who had been a part of the ceremony. On top of the stones are placed the last things she used — her plate and cup and utensils. On all

Tswana graves there are such dishes and plates, left there and never stolen or taken away. They lie there and rust and get old, but they stay there. The humblest grave is so dressed.

So we had this great funeral, and when it was finished we walked away in hundreds, down the little paths, through the village, everyone quiet and sad, going home, everyone totally immersed in a community sadness. The community ceremonies are the same: You don't send out invitations to anything. It is expected that the crowds will automatically come.

THE
BAKGALAGADI

The further out west you go, from Mochudi, the closer you get to the Kalahari Desert. On the edge of the desert live a people who have a half-half life: part hunting-gathering and part black. They are hunters and food gatherers, but they also keep goats and chickens. Not nomadic, like the Bushmen, but with well-made clay huts and village walls. They are very close to game, so they trap and hunt, but as they are right on the edge of the desert there is no way of growing anything. They are called the Bakgalagadi, "the in-between people." I have stayed with them many times, and we are good friends, although I cannot speak their language and they cannot speak mine. One of my close witchdoctor friends is one of them.

When I go out into these regions, I pass through the black villages, pick up a tracker, then go out to the Bakgalagadi on my way into the real desert to search for and live with the Bushmen. I once stayed with the Bakgalagadi to see and learn how much they had absorbed of the Western world, and it was a fascinating experience. They had begun to construct a school building (no thatch available, so no roof, but it hardly rains there, anyway); the classes met under a tree, with a piece of flattened cardboard box nailed up for a blackboard on which the teacher wrote with white chalk or charred wood. The children wrote with their fingers, in the sand. I used to tell them, "So lucky you are. You don't have to take books home and do homework to show your mother." In any case, their mothers probably couldn't read or write. They wore school uniforms bought from the black villages, which identified them as scholars, and they did a lot of singing and dancing, some arithmetic, and reading from the Bible. Not much more than that, but at least it was some education.

One day I said, "Let's sing and dance together. What instruments have you got? " There are no large trees, there, so I thought there couldn't be any drums, but I was wrong. They fetched a cow's skin that had been scraped and cleaned. A circle of them held it tight, one of them took a stick, and they had their drum! So simple, so effective.

I explained to the villagers how we had hand pianos (*mbilas*) in Venda. "Of course," they said. "We do, too." "Oh, no," I said, "it's not possible; you can't have those here. You haven't got the right trees" "Of course we have," they told me. They went away and got a rolled-up pack of wooden strips, the same size as the notes on a large *mbila* — about twelve inches in length, four inches across, with varying thicknesses for each note. They were strung together with leather thongs, and when they unrolled them I said, "Yes, those are the notes of the piano, but how will you play it?" They dug a trench in the hard, dry ground and strung the notes across the top and pegged them tightly to make them taut. In this way the trench became the soundbox, and they sat down on the sandy floor, took up two sticks each, and started to play. The sound carried across the desert, and it was beautiful. I couldn't believe I was listening to this musical form where one would imagine it impossible to create such an elaborate instrument. It just shows that you can overcome anything if the desire is there. I had assumed it couldn't be. Assumptions can be so wrong.

They play a variety of games, as well, which they were happy to show me. When oxen are yoked there are two wooden pegs on each side of the head, quite long pegs. These pegs are used for a game rather like horseshoes: You dig one peg into the ground, upright, then pace back some distance and use the other pegs to throw at the first one, seeing how close you can come to it. The Afrikaners used to play this game, which they called *jukskei*, on their Great Trek from Cape Town north into the interior. I joined in playing, one day, and to my horror found I was winning. As I was playing against the local headman, this was a disaster and I had to do something. It wouldn't do for the chief to lose face being beaten by a woman. I slowly made some mistakes, so as not to be too obvious, and all ended well. He was happy and said he would like to play with me some other time, but I could tell that that other time would never take place.

These people cannot speak a word of English, so long conversations were not possible, only halting questions. But communication comes not just through spoken language. I got to know some of them quite well and loved them for their warmth, kindness and friendliness. I also became friendly with their local *nyanga* (herbalist) and his wife, a gentle couple about forty-five or fifty years old. This man had lived his entire life in this area, in service to his people. He did not have a full bag of the different bones and utensils in his divination kit because so many items were not available to him there, but he had some bones and some dice carved out of animal horns and quite a variety of plants available to him.

The Bakgalagadi wear a lot of skins. They were very good at hunting and trapping and so could make *karosses* — skins sewn together with sinew, to form a warm blanket. They trapped all the pest animals — small wild cats, the black-footed cat, genet, mongoose, jackal, meerkat, and many other small rodents with fur. These animals were plentiful and provided a resource for the people to make clothing for themselves and also for sale, to make a living in an otherwise very poor area. They wore skin aprons as skirts and a sort of leather loincloth that went between the legs, up the back, and tied at the waist. Hard rawhide was the base for sandals, with soft hide for the ties. They made skin bags for food gathering and used skins to sit on, sleep on, and to carry babies on their backs.

I remember asking why they called their place *Kudumalapapwe* — the Valley of the Tortoise — when I had never seen one there. "Ah, Mashudu," they would say, calling me by my African name, "when the great rains come, then this place is alive with tortoises." They hibernate and stay under the ground until the conditions above ground are right. They are a great delicacy: The Bakgalagadi roast them in the fire, whole and alive. They must be placed on the hot ashes alive because as they die, they empty the bladder and intestines in their struggle and so clean themselves out. When cooked, they are opened up from the underside, the gall bladder is removed, and the rest of the meat can be eaten. It is terribly sad, but where human survival is extremely difficult it is understandable. The children catch tortoises and bring them home to be cooked and eaten, with the best bits handed round. The heart and head, considered special, may be given to their mother. There is always an ash fire smouldering, ready for such things to be cooked. Not a large fire with red coals, but a grey hot ash fire, from hard woods. The children know from their early years about anatomy; they know about the bile and to carefully remove the gall bladder.

THE BUSHMEN
AND THE DESERT LIFE

t was inevitable (I always dreamt of it); I just *had* to meet the Bushmen. Every year when Cecil and Uncle Johnny would off into the desert on hunting trips, I used to watch the trucks drive away with such a longing in my eyes. When would it ever be my turn? I was always pregnant in those days, and there was always a small baby to look after as well as the new one coming. I have had eight pregnancies but only reared five, having lost three. At long last came the time when I could go and leave my children with an aunt. This was in 1960.

We would pack up several trucks and bakkies [pick-ups] with provisions: forty-four gallon drums of water, forty-four gallon drums of petrol, bags of onions, potatoes, and oranges — so that we kept fit — and plenty of beer. A dear friend of mine, Louis, who could speak fluent Tswana, always went with me, plus some Tswana trackers who could read spoor [tracks] very well. We took them until we found a Bakgalagadi who came along who could read the spoor on the desert floor like a book. You don't just *find* the Bushman; you have to hunt for the recent spoor and follow it.

One time, Cecil gave me a kombi bus [a van] which is air-cooled and doesn't take water — a great asset in desert travelling. The kombi is high off the ground and so misses tree stumps and rocks, a very good vehicle for my kind of travelling. I used to take all the seats out, rope the drums of water and petrol behind the driver's seat, then add the boxes of provisions, plus extra engine parts, shovels and spades, an axe, cutting hooks, hammers and nails. I don't have a posh camp, but a working one — much more fun and it teaches how to survive in harsh conditions. My children thus all grew up with great ability in the bush.

In the very deep sandy areas, when the going is hard, you get four miles to the gallon of petrol. You have a long piece of hosepipe, and when you want to fill up the petrol tank, you place one end in the drum of petrol, suck hard to bring the petrol flow, and then quickly push the other end where the petrol goes into the tank. It flows well, once you've got the pressure going.

The truck is packed with each thing inside some other thing — no wasted space. No tinned food — it weighs too much. Lots of dried things you can soak overnight. Everything must be roped down. At the last village before entering the desert I would buy a live goat, or sheep if any available. The latter were scarce.

To prepare a whole sheep — to preserve the meat without refrigeration whilst on one's travels, cut up the sheep into large pieces — legs, thighs, sides, etc. — and soak the meat in a special sauce, to completely cover the meat. This sauce is made of vinegar, sugar, salt, herbs, spices, and oil. You can use white wine instead of the vinegar. This preserves the meat for a long time. I always took large pieces of mosquito netting with me, and once the camp was set up I hung the meat in a tree and made a cover all round it with the netting, to keep out the insects that might lay eggs in the meat. The net must not touch the meat but be like a large tent around it. The cool winds would blow through and around it and keep the meat fresh. The desert is hot in the daytime but really cold at night, so the meat cures nicely. The utensils that I took with me were not the things you usually use in a house but nails and hooks to fix into trees — to hang things on — and hammers and my special axe. I kept that axe sharp and used it myself. To prepare the evening meal, you take the axe and cut off a suitable piece of meat, and there you are — no refrigeration necessary. The meat never went off [turned rancid].

When we needed a live animal for food, it was killed with the swift cut of a sharp blade on its throat. Then I would skin it. This is one of my gifts – I am a very good skinner — and when finished there is not a mark on my skins. I also cut up the meat, knowing (as a nurse) the muscles and making the joints for hanging up in the tree. The liver can be used immediately, along with the other offal, and it is very good roasted on the open fire. The meat is better if hung overnight, after basting it with the same sauce I had prepared at home for the meat we brought along with us.

We didn't worry about wild animals getting to the meat in the desert because they were put off by the large white gauze tent. The lions certainly can smell the raw meat hanging in the tree, but we always slept with a good fire burning to keep animals away, and it worked. On one occasion we had a large male lion worrying round the camp all night. One of us got up and drove the truck towards it and around it for some time until it was frightened away. Mostly the animals kept away.

We could prepare meat in this way in the desert, but we couldn't have done that in Venda. Fortunately, we had refrigerators in Venda that worked on paraffin. They worked quite well, as long as we trimmed the little lamp to keep the insects out. If they were attracted to the light and fell in and died, the lamp would smoke and go out and the fridge stopped working. It was a constant job, every day, to trim the lamps for the house and the lamp underneath the fridge. I remember coming home from somewhere, once, and finding my house full of paraffin smoke because a moth had fallen in and died and put the fridge out. Very smelly.

In Botswana, outside in the yard underneath a shady tree, we had a kind of coolbox. This box was the same size and shape as a fridge, made of a wooden frame with double wire netting for the sides. Within the wire netting was coke from coal. The top was wood and over that draped several large sacks. Above this box was a container of water with a tap that dripped water onto the sacks, which then trickled down onto the coke, percolating through it and keeping the sacks wet all the time in spite of the dry atmosphere. As they were constantly wet and cool, with the breezes that blew through the place the contents of the food safe were kept fresh. I kept my butter, sausages, cheese, etc. outside there, in the yard, and they never went bad. (The butter would have melted in the house, so hot it was in there.) When we killed the weekly animal for the butcher shop, this is where I kept my meat, in this safe. So easy to construct and so efficient. But you had to bleed the meat first, and hang it, so it wasn't wet. We didn't use good clean water for keeping the sacks wet, but river water, which a young helper would fetch in a drum every day, rolling it up from the river and filling the small tank.

So, in all the different places that I lived, there was always a way to keep my family well fed, without any modern conveniences.

For our first night's drive into the desert — a long distance — I always had roasted chickens from home, wrapped in cloths and then in newspaper. These are the best insulators: Newspaper keeps food hot or keeps cold things cold.

I got to know that there are three different types of Bushman, with three different kinds of cultural patterns, three different languages, and in fact three different physical characteristics. The more I got to know about them, the more it became an obsession with me to meet them. I used to eat, sleep, and think about Bushmen; I wanted to know more and more, to do comparative studies with the Venda.

Sometimes when I stopped off in Kudumalapapwe I would find Bushmen there, looking after things for the blacks. I saw one man who would be perfect for me as a tracker. He had a half-half ability — both languages and both cultures. I always had with me a true Tswana as a companion, and on this occasion I said to him, "Let's take the Bushman; he's perfect. He knows it all and will find other Bushmen for us. It's better than taking a Bakgalagadi." The Tswana told me I would have to negotiate, but I asked, "With whom? Either he wants to come or he doesn't. I will pay him." "No, no, no," said my friend. "He doesn't make his decisions. He belongs to them. They will have to decide." "Don't tell me he's a slave," I responded. "Oh yes," I was told. "He works for and lives with them. He has no rights at all." I then had to sit down and spend a lot of time, discussing and working out how I could hire this man. I gave some presents of loose leaf tobacco— the natural leaf, straight from the land. I always carried certain items for gifts, as you never knew when such things would be necessary. Tobacco leaf was always a good gift because you could make snuff out of it or pound it up and smoke it. It doesn't grow there, so it is highly prized and greatly appreciated. Salt, too, is a super present, as they have none — only lime licks which the animals love, too. My Tswana companion did all the talking, whilst I — who was in charge — sat quietly, waiting for all to be arranged. Nobody is in a hurry because nothing much ever happens there — so, why make it happen quickly? The attitude is, this whole event is fun, so let's prolong it.

Eventually I learnt that I had bought the slave for a week at a certain price, which was paid to the owner. They had seen my truck and asked for onions and oranges — great luxuries — so we gave them all they required. I told the Tswana to assure the Bushman that he, too, would be paid. The Bushman had not expected that and was pleased at the bonus.

I certainly had not expected to find that situation and I don't know whether or not it still exists (with the Bushmen as slaves to the blacks), but no one seemed the slightest bit perturbed by the arrangement except me. The Bushman gained a nice week away with us, being well fed and paid, so he was happy. The owner was happy, and I gained a good tracker. But inside I found it sad and wrong.

Why doesn't the Bushman run away? For one thing, he is much smaller and has no weapons but bows and arrows. His owner is much bigger and stronger and has guns. The Bushmen are in a no-win situation: The Western world is encroaching into his desert and making it smaller, hunting all his animals, so it is difficult to find meat. The Tswanas go into the desert and sleep with the Bushwomen and produce half-half people, so they are losing their race. More and more land, with wells going down, is converted to cattle farms, so they are even losing their land. It is sad to see this happening to a proud and exceptional people.

Once we left the village and pushed into open country, right into the desert, we would start looking on the sandy floor for spoor marks in the sand, the story of the movement of people and animals plainly left — if you know how to read it.

The three groups of Bushmen are the !Kung, the G/wi and the !xong. The ! is a click sound. There are three places in your mouth where you click — forward, middle, and back — and most whites find it impossible to speak the click language. I cannot do it. The three groups speak three different languages. They have different ceremonies and approaches to God.

We left the sand roads, then the tracks, bumping, crashing through undergrowth over the bush country, taking care not to put a wheel into a hole. We went right out into the "nowhere" region. The trackers always watched from the back of the truck, looking at the sand for spoor. When I wasn't driving, I too sat in the back, on a piece of mat roped onto the water drums, from where I could see for miles and miles.

We took turns driving, as it is very heavy going and very tiring.

Many different people went into the desert with me, over the years. We enjoyed those trips and were always there to study. I was very particular about whom I chose to accompany me, because not everyone can be happy and live comfortably in such circumstances. I limited the number and interviewed them all at home, before committing myself. I would say, "First I want you to know that going into the Kalahari isn't just a holiday. It is hard work and you will play your role. I will find out what your gift is and you will do that as often as is necessary. You must understand that I am in charge of the trek. There has to be a leader: As in climbing a mountain, only one decision maker. In the desert it is exactly the same — only one person who says you may stop and eat, how much water you may have and how often. The trip's success rests on the leader. I am a nurse; I know how much one can take in difficult situations. You will accept the rules that I give. Are you prepared to come in under those controls?" A lot of people just said, "No, I'm not prepared to go on a holiday like that." "Ah," I would reply, "it's not actually a holiday, you see." But many came.

The trip can only last as long as the water lasts, and so the decision on when and how to use it and how much to use is very important. That is why I normally used a kombi, because they don't take water. The engine is air cooled. Whenever the engine was overheated, I would face it into the wind, open up the hood, and let the engine cool down. My early Botswana friends taught me things like that, all the survival stuff, the tips that become second nature. I learnt so much about how to make do and mend, and what to do when alone and without help.

There was a small aeroplane crash in the desert, one time, and the two occupants got out and started to walk for help. That is the last thing you do: You don't leave a large marker like a plane. You stay with it and wait for help, because people will start looking for you and will find the plane. An individual cannot easily be seen, certainly not from an air search. The more you walk in the desert the more dehydrated you become, and so you eventually die of thirst and dehydration. The people in the plane had nothing with them and were not prepared for walking, so they died. I don't think I would ever die there. My husband knew that and whenever I went in, even when I went alone, he felt confident.

In the same way, you never walk far from your camp unless you have a couple of oranges with you, because you can live without food for many days but you cannot live without liquid. If anyone set out for a nice walk we would always call out, "Here, take a couple of oranges."

On one trip I had a professor of toxicology from Pretoria with me and he said, "I'm taking your son Clive out walking, to learn about the toxic plants. So the very young boy and the elderly gentleman set out on their own, with no knife or gun, walking in the wilds. They were gone nearly all day. There are leopards and lions out there, but the ones that really scare me are the packs of wild dogs, as they don't just kill you, they rip you to pieces as they eat the bits of flesh.

It was getting to late afternoon and I began to worry about my son. I said to Cecil, "It will be dark in a few hours; I think I'll just take the truck and take an outing." He understood my concern and came with me to look for Clive. We found him and the professor, far from camp, sitting in some thorn thickets and hoping we would come, because a pack of wild dogs had found them. They were wise to sit still, protected by the thorns. If we hadn't gone to look for them they still could have survived. It would have been a bitter cold night, but one can survive cold without liquid. During the extreme heat of the day, here is what you do: Take off all your clothes and make a pile of dry grass under a thicket, in the shade. (Lions always rest in such places because they know about survival in the heat.) Urinate on the grass, then sit in it and keep it wet — urinating on it again, from time to time — because the wet grass will aid in keeping up your own body fluids. Urine is a clean substance and can do you no harm. It actually can help save your life. If you sit patiently in the wet grass, you do not dehydrate, and you can be found by trackers who can read spoor — even when the spoor is days old. People trying to find lost folk can always hire trackers to follow trails.

Of particular importance to the Bushman is the ostrich, whose large egg is the equivalent of twenty-four chicken eggs. The shell is used for collecting the rare rains, then is corked with dry grass and buried in the sand for emergency use. The Bushman can travel long distances with one egg shell full of water hanging in a skin bag tied round the waist. The shell is very thick and strong; you have to have a hammer to break it. These shells are also the material of the Bushman's only form of jewellery. They make beads out of the shell — a long and laborious process, taking months for one necklace. These necklaces are the Bushman's only item of inheritance. Everything else they possess is buried with them in the grave, but the necklaces go to their children.

The Bushmen dig a big hole in the ground and bury the dead in a sitting position with all his artifacts, so that his spirit will be properly equipped. They don't have ancestral spirit worship as the blacks do, but there is a spirit, and the family will never go back to that burial place again.

The first thing that struck me forcibly, when I started living with the Bushmen, was the complete lack of colour in their lives. Everything is brown — the skin clothes, the wooden artifacts, the hunting tools, the digging sticks, the wooden stamping blocks, everything. And yet, when the rains come, it is amazing how quickly the plants turn from brown to green and flowers which may have lain dormant for years suddenly bloom in a profusion of colour. It is like a miracle, but the rain is like nothing I have ever seen before — so heavy you cannot see properly. The accompanying wind is so strong that everything blows about. You can see these storms coming, but there is nothing you can do but wait them out: There is no place to go. In their delight over the long-awaited rain, the Bushmen remove their clothes and have a great natural shower. (When we had been in the desert for some time and were feeling all stinky and smelly, we did the same — and were grateful for it!) They take great pleasure in the new and colourful flowers and rush to gather them and push them into their tight, peppercorn hair, for adornment.

These flowers provide the only colour in their lives. There is no way they can use them to obtain a dye colour, but in any case what would they dye? They have only skins to wear. The desert is also the only place I know where there are no artificial stimulants — no tobacco, no wine or beer, no way to ferment anything.

Do they live long? No. The life is too hard. I have seen women in their late forties who looked like old, gnarled tortoises. Their skin dries up and wrinkles early. There is no fat in their diet, so they are thin and have dry, tough skin. Their bare feet are hard like a rhino's skin. I was able to ascertain the ages of women by talking for hours with them and dating years by events in the past — a locust invasion or drought or great fire. Then I knew roughly when they were born.

There are many kinds of food in the desert, but they are not all available all the time. At the time for *tsamma* melons, that may be the only thing they eat. The flying ants come out at the rains, and they hatch in thousands. In Sibasa (Venda) I would regularly see different hibernating insects suddenly appear. Out of holes in the ground they came — butterflies, flying ants, locusts. I remember seeing dozens of young Venda girls running in after the ants, kneeling down and grabbing them in handfuls, stuffing them into their mouths, not even waiting for them to die — wings and all. They also used to roast these insects. Likewise, in the desert, it is the food from the Bible.

The gum of the acacia tree is the Bushman's delicacy. As it runs down the side of the tree and hardens in strips, this "gum candy " glistens in the sun and catches the Bushman's eye. Up he runs to it, breaks off a piece, then chews with delight and a smiling face. Then they are like children in a candy store.

Among the Bushmen there is no chief, no headman. Everyone is equal in the decision-making and their survival depends on making the right decisions. Each person uses his own special gift for the benefit of the community.

The hunters and trappers fascinated me particularly. Making traps is quite an art. One day we went out to make traps from scratch, with nothing but a digging stick (their main tool, used for everything). They showed me which stick to cut down and how to find the sisal plant, for making rope. This, too, is a great art, but so easy once you know how. The trap will not be set just anywhere, but where the Bushmen have observed the daily passage of a certain animal. They know its habits and so choose the likely spot. Animals have set trails and territories, so you place the trap accordingly.

Once the trap is set, you break off branches and place them in the sand alongside the trap, to cover it up and make the area look like natural bush. Sure enough, the next day we had our animal. The boys use sticky gum from trees to make traps for birds.

The cooperation amongst these people gave me much to ponder about my own life and those of my children. Here, everyone works together to ensure the survival of the group. And, in spite of the desperate hardships, they all seem so happy. Whilst they do not sit down formally and have schools, their lives are daily lessons-by-observation. Sometimes I would go out with them on their early morning walks, when the women and their daughters spread out to cover as much ground as possible and the young girls received their basic training for life — food collecting, tracking, learning about babies and caring for them. I liked to take an interpreter along on these walks, as there was always so much to learn.

Whilst the female groups are out walking, the men teach the boys to hunt and trap. When I saw what fun it was, I asked them to teach my son, which they did, and then my daughters also wanted to learn, so we all ended up having a try. They made small bows out of soft wood with wild sisal for the string, and arrows with blunt ends. They taught their boys how to use these bows by shooting at set-up targets — seedpods, gourds, etc. My children found it very difficult to do, but the Bushman children were very accurate and could knock them down most times. For them it is not a game; it is survival.

The Bushman boys start hunting with these bows at age five learning about staying downwind of animals ("Which way is the wind blowing? Are you upwind or downwind? ") and about the kneeling-crawling approach, keeping bent well down, moving slowly and not rushing. The teachers are the old men, "the place of wisdom "as with the Venda. They hunt beetles just as intently as if it were buck. There are rhinoceros beetles, with two very big horns, and if you can find two large males you can watch an exciting beetle fight, with the two really going for each other. They are good for hunting lessons.

The children watch and learn each other's patterns of behaviour, because at some stage the boys will choose a hunting partner and they will probably hunt together for years. They must know how they will react when out on the hunt, because there will be no spoken instructions. They must know which role each one will assume, during a hunt, and each different animal's behaviour. They must be able to anticipate each nuance of movement, just as a pride of lions will do when out hunting.

This is a point I always make in my high school graduation speeches. I emphasise the importance of true friendship, which I hope they have learnt in school — the importance of being able to rely on one man or one woman in any circumstance. My husband had such a friend, who was like a blood brother until he died.

The Bushmen live in small groups of fifteen to twenty-five people. Their groups cannot be larger because they would eat up the natural resources too quickly. They cannot have great tribal villages, as the blacks do; it just wouldn't work. The group will get bigger or smaller with marriages and children. When daughters get married, they leave their group and move into the husband's band. Everyone in this society is absolutely equal— no chiefs, leaders, policemen, or anyone in authority. When they are going to move from one area to another they have a talk session, where everyone takes part. The decision affects them all, so they all decide.

In drought times, even the desert animals change: They do not get fertile, because it would be useless for them to produce babies when they could not support them. Nature, in its wisdom, sees to that. At those times everything and everyone is stressed and the line of survival is very slender.

We kept our fresh water in large drums and always made sure to have enough so that, even if we broke down, we could survive. One of the presents I used to give away, in times of drought, was water. Have you ever given anyone a gift of water and watched that incredible joy? Imagine, I would find a group of about seventeen people who hadn't had any real water in years — only fluid from roots and plants — and I would call my helper for a full bucket of clean, fresh water. I would place it in front of them and say, "That's yours." The adults hadn't seen any for so long, and the children had NEVER seen any! You can understand, but you cannot relate to such a circumstance. It really affected me. I cried.

The men came forward first and drank and drank until their stomachs bloated out round and full of water, so dehydrated were they. The hunters — the men — are the backbone of the group, so they drank first. But they didn't take just a little, or just enough; they took as much as they wanted, until they were full. Then came the fertile women, then the teenagers, then the older women — my age group, because we still have a use — and last the little children. Were the men concerned about how much there was and whether there would be enough to go round? No. That was not important. They just took what they wanted. Men and women are equal on vote-taking and decisions, but not on food distribution. They are fed according to their level — according to their importance to the group.

Speaking of food, I once had a great surprise whilst living with the Bushmen. In my hometown of Bristol, England, there is a local dish made of pig's blood and fat, poured into a long skin sausage. It is called blood pudding, and you cut it up in slices and fry it with bacon, apples, and onions. It is very good. I was brought up with that as a treat dish. In Venda they cook the blood in a pot but not made into sausages. The first time I saw a Bushman hunt a buck, I went off with the men and watched what they did with the animal: First they bring a pile of branches and lay them out to make a place to work on. (You cannot work on sand.) Then they lay the buck on the branches and slit open its belly and pull out its intestines, hanging them on a nearby little bush. They run their fingers down the intestines, squeezing all the contents out, leaving a long skin container.

Whilst one hunter works on the animal, the other hunter digs in the ground to make a sand hole like a bucket. They line this hole with skin, and so have a skin bucket in the ground. Now they remove the animal's stomach and empty it completely into the skin bucket and bend down and drink and suck up that nutritious content. Sometimes they place grasses over the top of the bucket and sieve the contents, so that only liquid falls into the bucket itself and they get a wonderful drink full of enzymes and minerals and healthy vitamins; then they eat the solid wet stuff on top of the grasses. This is only for the hunters, because no one else is there, at that point.

If there is a large dead tree near the kill, you can take an axe and chop the top clean and use that as a table to place the skinned buck on and chop it up. If they have somewhere suitable to place the meat, they can use the wet, bloody skin just off the killed animal to line the sand hole, as it is soft and pliable, when wet, and fits easily into the hole. When they have drunk all that good stomach juice, then the skin is used to wrap up all the meat, offal, liver, etc. All those soft meats are for the people with no teeth — the very young and the very old.

Now the hunter really squeezes and cleans out all the yards of intestines, hanging it back on the bush as he goes. He then bleeds the buck's blood into the intestines, cutting a major vein to do so, until all the blood is out and caught to make a blood sausage, just as they do in Bristol! Can you imagine? I can't tell you how excited I was with this discovery! It only proves my belief that there are so many similarities in life, and so few differences. And of course, this food is perfect for the grannies and the babies — high in protein — as you don't need teeth to eat it. This blood sausage, and all the meat, is cooked in the fire — nothing is eaten raw. The blood would firm up naturally but the baking in the ashes also sets it, so you can cut off little pieces. They roll it into little bits and put it into a young child's mouth for a healthy meal.

The two men are kept very busy skinning, cutting up and sorting the buck, because they must get it back to the camp and they may have come far. If it is too far to carry the meat, then one of them goes back to tell the group and they all move over, make a temporary home, and live next to the buck until it is all gone.

In everything the Bushman does he is quite clean — not with water, because he doesn't have any, but with urine, which cleans his hands beautifully.

Even in my excitement, however, I have never eaten the Bushmen's blood pudding, as it really isn't clean in our terms. The difficulty of crossing cultural barriers is that there are inevitably a few no's. I haven't been born to withstand the kinds of bugs they have. It probably would kill me if I just ate everything.

One year I did decide to eat as much of their food as I possibly could, as I had a medical friend who was on that trip. He photographed and studied insects, but I asked him to take every kind of medicine to fix my stomach, if necessary — which he did. That meant I could take some chances. Nobody else did. I was the only one to eat what the Bushmen ate. I don't mind getting intestinal or stomach problems, normally, but if I am the only driver and have to keep the camp going, then I cannot take chances. On this particular trip, with others to help, I decided to experiment. And oh boy, did I suffer!

I lay in my sleeping bag on the sand floor, doubled up with pain, my intestines growling and grumbling with the unnatural stuff I had consumed. I would groan, and the diarrhea wouldn't stop, and I got dehydrated. I really paid for my experiment. I kept taking tincture of opium, which does help, and my dear Cecil would walk past me — lying there in pain — and laugh. I would say, "I'm dying. I'm dying." "Well, what a wonderful way to go," he would say. "Mad you are!" But he knew I would be all right. I did learn just what the Bushman diet really is — rough, fibrous plants, so indigestible, with sand on everything. Their teeth are filed down with the constant sand inevitably eaten every day.

LIFE IN THE
VELDT

W hen I'm in the desert I like to sleep under a small tree or bush. I put down a sheet of canvas, if I've brought some, or — if not — some dried grass makes a good dry place to put your sleeping bag. The desert sand at night is bitter cold and strikes up into your back. A sleeping bag alone is never sufficient. You would think, in the daytime, "Oh, I'll just lie down in this nice warm sand, " but comes the setting of the sun and it's a different story: ice cold. And the wind is not nice.

We always had sacks of onions, potatoes, and oranges, so having unpacked them and stored them away, we used the sacks. (I always had a big tin trunk in which I kept the food, away from insects and small animals.) Using thorns from the bushes, you sew them all together with string, to make a windbreak. Place sticks in the ground and tie the sackcloth onto them and you have a wonderful way to keep the wind away from where you sit round the fire.

In every camp, whether a one-night or a settled camp, you always dig a trench for rubbish. Then, when you move on, you rake the sandy soil and leave the area as you found it. If you leave anything lying around, like plastic bags, the animals can choke to death licking the tasty stuff on the bag and then swallowing the plastic. You burn what you can and bury the rest. Where you go out to make a toilet, you take a spade and bury the excreta.

We always dig a second trench which we line with sacks and fill with cans of beer. Every scrap of water used — for cleaning vegetables or washing up the dishes, or even the cooled water from cooking potatoes — gets poured over the sacks to make them really wet on top of the beer. During the night the water will get very cold and make the beer cans cold. This is an easy way to chill things — refrigeration is not necessary.

When we had all the children in the camp and dinner was ready, I would call them all together for a wash. Knowing how scarce and precious the water was, they learnt to stand in a tight circle with their hands to the centre, one above the other. I would give a piece of wet soap to the top hands, which would be passed down from one to the other, then a mug of water was poured slowly over them all, to cascade down the hands, so that everyone got clean with only a few ounces of water. An enamel basin placed on the sandy floor would catch the water as it was poured, so that even that dirty soapy water from all those hands could be used again — on the sacks, to keep the beer cool. Even that was not its last use, as once it filtered though the sackcloth it went into the sand and gave life to a tree or bush.

At one particular campsite lived a large pack of baboons. It was a family group — one huge male, a lot of females and children, and young males. A good-sized group, for survival. I got to know them well over a period of about twelve years, as I loved the valley where they lived. In the cool of the evening they would come down from the caves on the hillside, on their way to the riverbed, where the water sipwells were.

You don't play games with baboons. They can be dangerous, and I never take guns with me. At the most I had my axe, for firewood, and a sharp knife, but even with those things there isn't much I could do if a baboon ever attacked me. Some of them are big, so you don't do stupid things. If I had visitors or children with me, I would advise everyone to come into the camp area near the fire at around 5:00 PM, because the baboons would be coming down soon. On one of my first trips, I felt the animals were too close for comfort and wondered whether they could undo the zip on a sleeping bag, but I soon learnt that they do not come too close to any fire, so that was our protection. We always kept a fire going all night.

THE MOON DANCE
OF THE BUSHMEN

T he moon is a prince to the Bushman — a great god — and every single month they pay tribute to him and dance and sing. This is one of my favourite ceremonies and I asked if I could take part, even though I was a woman. I actually wasn't sure that they knew I was a woman, as I am a bit strong and tough and in the desert I wore trousers. They also saw me getting on and off the truck and wielding an axe, so I tried to explain and said to the women, "Look, I'm like you" and pointed to my bosoms. Then I asked, "Can I dance with the men? " Among the Bushmen, the women stand in a row and trill a melody and clap their hands whilst the men dance. The women provide a percussion beat and the rhythm.

They said I could dance, that it would not upset any gods because I was different (white) and not one of them, so there was no problem. Their god is called !Ndimo.

We stood in a line about a metre apart — six men with me at the end. In Venda all dances take place in circles, large or small, but not so here in the desert. Here, it is not communal dancing; each man has his spot and he stays on it, dancing and jumping up and down in the same place. Gradually he makes a depression in the sand, getting in deeper as he dances — a bit like dancing in a sand pit. I didn't get too close to them but stood off to the side. Wherever I go I am careful not to break any ethnic taboos or barriers, or upset any patterns of behaviour.

They have no musical instruments because there isn't much available in the desert to make them. Throughout my nine years of visiting them I saw only a few — no reeds and no drums, no gourds for soundboxes. I saw only small stringed instruments, made from sinew and pieces of trees, like a one-string violin.

Whilst we were dancing the fire was burning and the men were singing and grunting. I grabbed my interpreter to find out what they were saying. The song is to the moon, to say thank you to him: "Please, we love you; you are so beautiful, please come back. " They don't take the moon for granted, as we do; they pay him tribute every month. The moon is their only light. When he is gone their world changes. I remember how they would come round our campfire at night and look at our paraffin lamps and torches [flashlights]. These were unknown to them.

So the Bushmen would say goodbye and know that the moon was going and that there would be no more dancing at night. They don't have candles or any form of fuel, so they rely entirely on the moon. At least the black people have other resources.

BUSHMAN PAINTING

Having studied their culture for so long, I was curious to learn whether the ability the Bushmen had when they painted rocks all over South Africa hundreds and thousands of years ago still existed in today's Bushmen. Not for engravings — because they live in the desert, now, rather than in the great mountains where they once chipped designs into rock with primitive tools — but for paintings, as in those still visible throughout the country inside caves and under rock overhangs.

I took sketching pads and pastel crayons of the right colours the Bushmen would have used (white, black, reddish brown, golden brown, all the colours from Nature). I carefully marked the paper's "top" and "bottom" and identified the artist — by sex and age — so I would know which way up the picture was supposed to go and whose interpretation it was — a woman food gatherer or a male hunter. I had a very good interpreter with me that year, so communication was 100%.

I learnt that the Bushman's powers of concentration for this sort of thing are very limited — after twenty minutes or so they were bored and got up and walked away. So I worked with them a little bit at a time, very slowly and over many days, to get a good cross-section of drawings from a good number of the group.

Having marked the paper for identification, I would place it in front of the person and — first showing him how to use them — placed the crayons by his hand.

When I said, "Draw me a lion," what I should have said was, "What does a lion mean to you?" Then they would draw eyes and spoor feet, because lions move at night and the Bushmen meet them, for the most part, at night, as eyes, and they know how to read the lion's spoor. They didn't draw the eyes inside the lion, but outside, emphasising the importance of those large yellow glaring eyes. Likewise, when they drew an animal with stripes, the stripes would be separate on the page. They drew whatever was important to that particular animal, what they remember relating to it, what it meant to them. All the strangeness of the rock paintings suddenly made sense to me.

I have seen paintings of a buck that we thought were of a dead buck, lying on its side, but it is not a dead buck — only their interpretation of a buck, showing all its four legs. In black art it is common to show everything — all four legs, or two arms, or two eyes. Just as in Egyptian art, where people may be in profile but there are two eyes side by side on that side of the face close to you, to say, "yes, this person did have two eyes."

In the early days of advertising, in South Africa, my black friends asked me, "This person sitting sidewise with one eye, advertising a face cream, is it only for one-eyed people? Or, if you show only one leg, then is the product for cripples?" We used to sell peanut butter, in our store in Sibasa, that had a label with a picture of a black cat and the words, "Black Cat Peanut Butter." I noticed that the blacks bought the other brand, with a different name, and when I asked why, they said, "You see that label? It says the peanut butter is made of black cats." When I explained that it was a company logo, they said, "Oh, no. Look at the can of peaches, or fruit jam. Look at the label. It has a picture of what is inside."

So their drawings are very literal. They show what is important to them. The tracking of animals is most important, so what they draw most is the spoor. Once when I asked a man to draw a snake, he drew not the snake but the wavy slither movement it makes in the sand. Then I tried the same thing with the women: I took my tin teapot and stood it on the sand with a cooking pot next to it. I put them not on a table — they don't have tables — but directly on the sand. Everything they do is at flat ground level. As they regularly see things from above when they are standing up, they drew the cooking pot as a circle with a smaller circle inside and a dot for the handle on the lid. They drew it from above. When I asked, "What about this?" and drew it our way, from the side, with the handle actually sticking up, they said, "What is that?" not recognising it from my visual perspective. The interpreter took ages explaining that I had drawn the same thing, and I would hold up the pot and show them the outline I had drawn, and eventually they saw it. It was so interesting. Their entire perspective was related to one flat plane.

A BIRTHDAY
WITH THE BUSHMEN

O n one trip I wanted to teach my children the differences between their lives and those of the Bushman children. Normally, my rule was that a child had to be twelve years old before making such a trip, but in this case I made an exception for the youngest two. Melody, my fourth child, was nearly ten at the time. She had begged, "I'm ready, I'm ready, please take me," and the older children told us, "She is ready, let her go." That left Natalie, the fifth one, who was eighteen months younger. What to do? We couldn't leave just one behind. Over the years of listening and watching the others and hearing so much about the desert they knew quite a lot about it, and as they had been in camping situations elsewhere we decided to take them along. It was only the desert that worried me a little with the younger ones.

The older three talked to the two little ones and said, "Now there are rules, and you must be aware of what this holiday is like. It's different. You can't have a drink of water until the leader says, and everything is rationed and served out according to proper controls. You have to work and do certain jobs." The little ones understood and agreed.

I decided I would give Melody a birthday party in the desert, as she was just a few days off being ten years old, and I took an iced birthday cake with us. Normally, I never took sweets or sweet biscuits, sugary cool drinks, or anything that gave you a thirst, for obvious reasons. Fruit squash does not quench your thirst; if anything, it makes you more thirsty.

I packed balloons and other party things, and off we went. Melody and Natalie had to travel with the other children on the back of the truck on top of the goods, in the blazing sun and heat. I sat with them, on top of the petrol tin. Cecil suffers from the sun so he travels inside the cab and shares the driving with our black driver, Mukluhelwa. The children were marvelous all the way in, with no complaints from anybody. I can see them now, in my mind, the little ones falling asleep on top of the truck, wedging their little bodies in between boxes and packages, to make a place and give us no problems. What a trip that was!

Once in the camp we organised the four girls inside the tent, and Clive, Cecil and I stayed round the fire. I had taken in tennis balls and a soccer ball, so we could have games, and the children went to find their Bushman friends. Catching a ball was quite impossible for the Bushmen, as in their lives they don't catch anything, but throwing was a different story. Clive threw a tennis ball at Aethcloudu, a young hunter about twenty years old. The hunter picked up the ball and threw it back, hard with deadly accuracy. He was a natural: He threw the ball like a spear. I said to Cecil, "If only I could get them to the Olympics, they would be a sensation." To kick a soccer ball was absolutely impossible for them. In anything related to natural hunting, they were brilliant; otherwise they had no coordination. On the day of her birthday, Melody woke up knowing it was her day but not expecting anything. As she came out of the tent she found her birthday cake on a cardboard box in a cleared area and balloons tied on all the thorn trees. We sang "Happy Birthday" and told her she could invite all the Bushman children to come to her party.

The Bushman children couldn't believe the cake. It was an iced fruitcake, so it was very pretty. Of course they had never seen or tasted anything like it before, but they knew me well and knew they could trust anything I gave them to eat. They were used to the sweet gum from the trees, so after they first licked the cake and found out its taste, it was instant magic. It disappeared just like that! But they had not rushed forward to grab it. They were accustomed to a definite order of food distribution and waited patiently for their turn.

When the cake had been completely finished, I said to Melody, "Take the balloons off the trees and start the games we usually play." What a sight it was! Every time a balloon was caught on a thorn tree and popped, the hunters and all the rest of them tried to find it. They couldn't believe where it was gone and couldn't believe that a little scrap of rubber was all that was left. We all remember that occasion to this day. It was very special for all of us.

That night we lay in our sleeping bags, looking up at the stars and identifying the constellations and thinking of the Bushmen and how close they are to all of Nature. We listened to the night noises. "What's that?" I would ask. Clive and Felicity knew; they had heard it before, so it was for Melody to identify. She got it right: It was a jackal. A coughing sound will be a leopard. But when you hear lions out hunting, that is special. The roars really go right through you. You begin to wonder, "How near are they? Will they come close?" The night is so noisy — full of insects and animals and their nocturnal sounds. A desert is not empty, and there is so much to learn.

The next day I said, "You've had your fun; I want to work today. You all can come and learn also. Today I want to learn to make fire with the Bushmen." My interpreter had explained that I wanted to learn to make fire right from scratch, from the very beginning. Once they knew that we wanted to do this, their reaction was beautiful — only a pleasure, they wanted to give their gift to us. Like you would take someone into your kitchen and teach them your best recipe.

So, my whole family of seven plus my interpreter, my tracker and the male Bushmen walked out into the bush. They showed us which bushes we would need — one with a hard wood, so we all cut a stick from that one, and another with soft wood, and we all cut another from that. In the soft wood we had to cut a small round hole in which the hardwood stick would be placed and rotated in our two hands. You create a black charcoal effect: The hard wood rotating fast in the hole makes it smoulder. They showed us which dry grass to collect — not just any grass — and that is placed round the smouldering to catch the spark. We all did this whole exercise and tried over and over, twirling our hands on the stick, making it rotate in the hole, but with no success. We were hopeless. Although we watched carefully and tried to copy them exactly, no luck. The only one of our group who finally got the wood to smoulder and the grass to catch (and as it catches you gently pick up the ball of smoking grass and give it a gentle blow to bring on the flame) the only one to achieve all that and make fire was little Melody. What a birthday present that was! Our little firemaker. On and off the whole day we worked hard and tried again and again, but Melody was the only one with the knack. We had cut the sticks right; that was no problem. Then the Bushmen encouraged us, showing us how to hold the bottom stick with our feet. Of course we couldn't do that. We couldn't even make the tiniest little ember — which they achieved every time. Very easy — if you know how.

Women never make fire; it is only for the men, and they are the ones who make the firesticks and carry them in their hunting bags. If they go away hunting, they must leave a fire going, because the women cannot make fire. Always there is a smouldering grey ash fire for the women to use, because the men could be gone for two or three days, hunting. They didn't mind that we women worked at making fire, because we are different and have different gods and taboos. In fact, when we got back to Johannesburg, Melody became known at school and elsewhere as the little girl who could make fire. One day there was a demonstration at one of the local archaeological sites where university professors were lecturing about the Bushmen, and one of the men phoned to ask if Melody would demonstrate this special ethnic practise. By this time she was seventeen years old, an elegant young woman, but she did it — and there is a wonderful picture of her, sitting in jeans and shirt, making fire with her sticks! All the cameras were clicking away at this phenomenon, because none of the blacks could do it.

That particular trip was a cross-pollination of ideas and cultures, with particular emphasis on their children and mine. Colette and Felicity, the two older girls, gave a hug goodbye to the young hunter, Aethcloudu, as the three of them had become very friendly during this trip. He, too, has probably not forgotten that special time when he had two admiring beautiful blonde girls as friends for a short while. It was indeed special for all of us.

Aethcloudu had his own lovely wife, so he wouldn't have pined much for my girls. Bushmen marry only one wife — unlike blacks, who can and often do have several. For the Bushman, life is too hard and food too difficult to find. To support one family is enough for them. They have one wife and no form of contraception, but they must not make their wife pregnant whilst she has a suckling child. The mothers breastfeed their babies for up to two years. There is no other food for the very young, so breast milk is essential. Bush families are small and compact, and they work. It is a question of survival of the fittest, because the weak don't live. If a man makes his wife pregnant by mistake, whilst she is suckling her child, he is regarded as a weak, selfish, and stupid man. When the pregnancy advances, her milk will dry up for the first baby, which is an impossible situation, and the mother must carry the baby on her back, which she cannot do with two. So the father will be frowned upon for doing that to her.

Bushmen must have children only when it fits their life pattern. In times of drought, when Nature controls the animals and they are not fertile, when plant food is scarce for man and animal alike, this is not the time for the Bushman to have babies either. In the bad times they are not even fit. I would come across a whole group with white fungus caps on their heads — a deficiency disease, from malnutrition. It is not infectious and will disappear once they get a better diet and the vitamins they were short of.

In Bushman society they hardly ever kill each other. No wars. They would rather talk it out. They are great talkers and love to talk things out. But there is one time when it is accepted as completely right that you may kill: if another man makes your wife pregnant. That is taboo.

I used to try to give a few lectures to raise money before I went into the desert, to buy multi-vitamins and other simple medicines for the Bushmen. When I arrived there and found a medical problem — a child very malnourished, for instance — I would ask my interpreter to say that I had a present for this child. Then, pointing to the sun, I would place one tablet in the child's mouth and say that every time the sun comes up they should do this. I managed to get many of them to take multi-vitamins and tried to provide enough to last long after I had gone, until some plants came back again to provide them with food.

Once I took in cartons of dehydrated vegetables to improve their food. I boiled a huge iron pot of water and cooked the vegetables to make a nourishing soup mixture. We gave this to every man, woman, and child, and how they enjoyed it! But the next day we learnt they had all suffered diarrhea from it — they just couldn't digest it.

MOZART
AND THE BUSHMAN BABY

One year I took my tape recorder into the desert with me. I taped the Bushman speech — fascinating, because there are three different Bushman languages, and each interprets the clicks their own way. They watched the delight in my face as I listened to them speak and taped their conversation and their music. Having taped them, I then played it back to them and they recognised their own voices.

I asked my interpreter to explain to them that where I come from we have music that is played on lots of instruments all at the same time and that I wanted them to sit and listen. I played them a tape of a Mozart piano concerto, some of my favourite music. There was a stunned silence. No conversation, no laughing, nothing. I did it all again the next day, the same procedure as before: first their music, then mine. But I couldn't get a reaction out of them, just polite quietness.

I had had greater success with other things, as we studied each other and our two cultures. They would approach and touch us, as a sign of friendship and bonding, and would touch and explore our clothing — buttons, pockets, etc. — in fascination. Once they felt our acceptance, they really started looking at all our things.

When they found the mirror on the truck and saw their own faces, it was incredible. They had never seen their faces before and didn't realise it was themselves. At first it was difficult for us to understand their confusion; then we realised they don't even have a large pan [pond] of water for reflections, where they would see themselves. So how could they know what they look like? Then we started showing them: "Look, look. See me. Now, see me in there." We will never know whether they comprehended it was them or whether they thought it was their spirits.

Years later, in 1972, we had an American Field Service scholar living with us. At our daughters' school they had asked if anyone would like a house-sister for a year and Colette had said she would. When she asked me, I said, "You mean you haven't enough sisters already?" but she was so keen to have an American sister her own age that we agreed.

We were meant to show Debbie all about South Africa, so I decided to take her into the desert. We told the family we were going in but everyone else had other commitments, so we two went in alone. We set off in my kombi and had a really interesting trip.

Whilst we were there, we heard there had been a baby born further away, with a Bushman group I did not know. We took the kombi, left camp, and followed the spoor until we found this other group. I had never seen a newborn Bushman baby, so I was very excited.

Whenever you make a camp and stay with one group, the word gets round and others just arrive. How they hear, I don't know, but it usually happens. I remember going to sleep, once, with seven Bushmen in camp, and waking up and finding eleven! They walk long miles in the cool of the night. They had heard I was there and they just arrived and moved in. The whole time they stay with me, they know they will be well fed and that they will receive water, so it's a holiday for them.

On another occasion, I found three new men in the morning, from the most remote part of the Kalahari Desert. They had walked through heavily populated lion country and they told us the tale of how they had to climb these little trees with lions all round them. The trees would rock because the lions were rubbing against them! They had had the most frightening trip, but there was so little food where they came from, they were looking for a place where their whole group could move. What was particularly exciting for me was their faces — very Mongoloid, Eastern faces, different from any other Bushmen I'd ever seen.

On the occasion I was in the desert with Debbie, a Bushman just appeared to tell us about the baby, so of course we went to see it. I took as a present small, colourful glass beads and some salt. When I leave any group I always give them beads, as there is so little colour in their life and they love them.

I was surprised to find a small round grass house in the camp, as I know they don't usually make houses, only windscreens. This was the first straw house I had ever seen. Normally, they build a half-moon structure with sticks in the ground, filled in with grass to make it windproof. The fire is placed at the end, so they lie down to sleep within the half-circle with their feet by the fire. They are then safe from lions. Bushmen do occasionally get eaten by lions, but by lying in their skins within this skerm, they are usually safe and away from the cold wind. They make dents in the sand, wrap themselves in their skins, and lie close to each other to keep warm. So, knowing all this, I was amazed to see this little hut. They are nomadic, so why bother with all that effort, I thought. The windbreak always seemed sufficient. This hut was like a large basin, upside-down.

It turned out the hut is made only for a pregnant woman. It is made of bent sticks with dried grasses tied all over. The woman goes to live in it near the end of her pregnancy. When she has the baby she goes out away from everyone and digs a hole, squats over it, and delivers the baby down into the hole. When all the placenta and blood has finished, she will bury that, then go back and live in her little hut for three months. No man in the group can see her during that time, not even her husband. You get help if you need it, when you have your first baby, but afterwards, no. If the first delivery is difficult and the baby not coming, they tie a thong round the stomach and pull it downwards to assist. There is a root that is full of liquid that you use at such times for cleaning up — just squeeze it and rub the baby and yourself clean. This root is available but not plentiful. Knowing she was going to have a baby, they all will have looked for and collected that root.

Without realising it, by keeping her isolated at that vulnerable time, she is ensuring that she and the baby will not pick up any infection. She is completely isolated from everyone except the women who bring her food. Nobody goes into the hut with her. It is far too small, anyway.

When I arrived at the camp the baby was about a month old. The whole group was standing round, expecting me. Someone did a test, once, on Bushmen's hearing capabilities and found they could hear trucks and aeroplanes sixty miles away, so acute is their hearing. I hadn't been camping many miles away, so obviously they knew all about my presence there and had heard my truck coming to their camp. I greeted them and smiled and did my usual friendly touching and talking — in English, but what does it matter? They could hear the tone of my voice.

The Bushmen always stay quietly and accept intrusions, because no matter who comes they will always be more powerful than the Bushmen, who are very little people. When hunters see you coming they hang up their bows and arrows, spears and sticks and step out towards you with nothing. It is the most disarming thing you will ever see in your life — literally showing, "Here we are at your service. What do you want?"

When I saw this group, suddenly I recognised someone. "Hi," I said, "I know you. How are you? What a pleasure! I believe there is a new baby, here." And I held my arms together and rocked them, as if I held a child. So it was OK for Debbie and me to go towards the hut to see the baby. We knelt down next to the hut and I spoke. "Please tell her I have brought the baby a present, and may I see the baby?" And from within the hut came the mother's voice. "What's she saying? Oh, please, what is she saying?" I asked. "She says that she knows you. She has never forgotten some years ago, in another place, that dreadful music that you brought"! That had been two years before, but she had never forgotten it, because to her it was cacophonous. I had played lovely Mozart and Beethoven to that group, but for two years she had never forgotten how much it disturbed her.

I gave her the gifts of beads, salt, and fresh water. Of course the water was a real gift, especially as she was breastfeeding. She welcomed us inside the tiny hut, and there she was, just sitting there like a beautiful statue, surrounded by skins on the floor. I looked at her and said, "I'm so happy to see you," and with grace she lifted a skin and pulled it back and there lay a perfect little girl of golden brown colour.

WITCHDOCTORING

We left Sibasa in January 1957 to come to Johannesburg for schools for our daughters. Felicity was almost seven and ready for school; Colette was five and Melody two. I couldn't just start placing the girls in boarding schools, as I had done with Clive, because I knew then I would see very little of any of my children. Clive came home only for school holidays. In between, I heard nothing from him, as he couldn't read or write when he left home. When we reached Johannesburg, I asked his school if he could now live at home, but they said, "No; once a boarder always a boarder," so he remained living at school until he was seventeen years old.

Prior to 1957 I was fully aware of the witchdoctors' ceremonies. Occasionally we saw a witchdoctor going somewhere with a goat or a white cock. I was allowed to watch a little bit but never to dance or take part or really learn anything. I kept asking, "When are you going to allow me to understand everything?" but was told no, that I didn't "belong" yet. I said, "Well, how long does it take to belong? I've been with you for ten years and do everything else." "Yes, that's a long time, but you are not one of us." I didn't, yet, have my black name, then; I wasn't yet a true member of their tribe. Many of them loved me dearly, but I wasn't a member. So I gave up. I loved watching, listening, and hearing the music, but I gave up the idea of becoming a witchdoctor, for the time being.

When Professor John Blacking introduced me to their music and culture, that was great, because I could see and take part in that. But the medicine was a closed book. The Venda women would show me the herbs, the berries, the bark from trees, leaves, and many roots, but they didn't tell me anything. The two main problems there are diarrhea in the babies, who die from dehydration, and constipation in the old folk who eat so much mealie meal porridge — heavy starch. Ralushai, who lived opposite my house, had roots he would boil and bottle the water — one kind for the babies, the other for the old people. He would mix powders with ashes and fat (brain or marrowbone from a goat) and make a cream substance to spread on nasty tropical sores. When I saw that, it made me think back to penicillin, that natural substance which was a gift from Nature also. I used to say to Ralushai, "You know, they do that in England; not exactly the same, but certainly natural things, from Nature. It all makes sense."

One day I was sitting with him, watching everything that was happening, and a man came along and sat down. He talked with my herbalist friend who handed him a bone flute to blow — made from the leg of an eagle, with one hole in it, so one note. The man blew the flute once, paid Ralushai tenpence, and then left. You don't rush things, in Africa, so I took a little time and then asked Ralushai what that was all about. "Why did he pay you money just to blow the flute?" "Oh, please," he said, "he has problems, that man — problems with his wife. They fight all the time and he is very unhappy. He is broken and he can't sleep; his spirit is in pieces." "But," I said, "tenpence for the flute: What did that do?" "The flute is made from an eagle, so tonight he will sleep, and when he sleeps he will dream and his spirit will soar on high like the eagle, and his problems will disappear."

I said, "You know, Ralushai, they have a man just like you in America, and he is called a shrinkhead [psychiatrist]. He helps people with their problems, only he charges a lot more than tenpence. But it's the same — the psychology is the same." So obviously I fell more and more in love with this dear old man and I spent many hours with him asking, "How did you do that?" "Why that?" "What is this?" "Tell me."

"Well," Ralushai would say, "here we have plenty storms, plenty big lightning, much fire; many huts burn down every year. So we have to appease the spirits. How do we do that? Come." After heavy rains, after a real tropical electric storm with sheet and fork lightning, we walked and collected "eggs from the sky" — toadstools. They are deadly poisonous, and I said, "Hold on; why are we collecting poison?" "Wag 'n bietjie," he replied. This is an Afrikaans expression meaning "wait a bit," but everyone uses it.

We baked the little eggs from the sky and then pounded them into a powder and placed them in a container — a gourd or bag. Almost everything to do with this profession must come from Nature. You store this powder until someone requires you to come and fix his hut. Then a ceremony takes place to make the hut safe from all this great lightning. You must see this lightning — in forks and sheets — playing all over the heavens. It comes in such great flashes that you could read a book, it is so light — and very scary. With really impressive thunder, as only Africa can produce. I have stood in my house with fires raging in the veldt scores and scores of miles away, with red heavens reflecting the fires — quite scary, and you pray that the wind will keep the fire's path away from your house. Once the whole of the low veldt was on fire, hundreds of miles away, and we could see the reflection in the sky. That is the Lord's way of creating fertiliser, because after the next rain the veldt comes alive with bright green shoots everywhere, and the blackened trees come alive with green leaves. The contrasts of Africa are great.

Obviously the people have great respect for fire and worry about their huts, made of sticks and straw roofs. Ralushai would go round the hut, sprinkling the powder and chanting. The powder would be used to keep the power of fire away from this hut. The power from the sky that grows overnight (the eggs from the sky) must be powerful enough, also, to keep it away. A ring of security.

The question is, Does it work? Sometimes; not always. What would the people say, if it didn't? "Oh well, it wasn't strong enough, this time, to keep away the fire." The medicines don't work 100%, but then they don't work 100% in white medicine either. So Ralushai wouldn't have any difficulty — he would have an out. He could say, "Yours was a particularly strong one; my medicine was not strong enough." The people are very warm in accepting the service of this profession without expecting miracles and always success. They do not criticise it too much, but accept the good and the bad. Maybe you have not been fully supportive to warrant full success; maybe you are not reading well. There is no aggression. In fact, my witchdoctor teachers are the most gentle, levelheaded people. They always say to me, when things go wrong, "Don't get so aggressive; accept things more." Sometimes, if a white person makes an appointment to see my teacher and at the last moment panics and doesn't pitch up, doesn't even phone or anything, I get angry and say, "Why did they do that?" but my teacher will say, "Don't worry; they are the losers. We have gained an extra half-hour together. Just calm down, Mashudu." (Mashudu is my Venda name, meaning "the lucky one." Often I am greeted as Mashudu Muratho, "Mashudu, the bridge." The honorary title bestowed on me by the Venda chief, for my service to his country, is Makhadzi and means, literally, "my sister by another mother.")

It is a much more balanced attitude to life, and an acceptance of circumstances that we busy, busy whites find intolerable. There is such wisdom in this profession.

So I learnt small bits of information, in Venda, but nothing of substance for witchdoctoring.

Top: *A sangoma.* Bottom: *Petras, the diviner who assisted Rae through her inauguration ceremony, with his three wives and some of his children.*

Nellie Mbara, the sangoma whose school Rae attended. At top she is with her husband; below she dances with another sangoma, wearing the characteristic black ostrich feathers with pink.

TOP: *Nellie Mbara, Rae Graham, and a herb gatherer.* BOTTOM: *A sangoma in a muti shop.*

TOP: *Nellie Mbara with her bones.* BOT-TOM: *Ndora faces the camera as she dances with two other women divin-ers. They have no black skirts as they are not sangomas.*

TOP: *Petrus Nemaungani, the witchdoctor who tested Rae over a period of five days to decide whether she would be given training.* BOTTOM: *Simon, a wizard.*

TOP: *The herd from which Rae bought a goat for her ceremony.*
BOTTOM: *A complete witchdoctor's costume.* FACING PAGE, TOP: *Rae (Mashudu) working at Ndara's kraal.* FACING PAGE, BOTTOM: *Mashudu's kit.*

TOP: *On the left, Mashudu's great herbalist teacher Ndora Thivhusiwi. In the center, Nellie Mbara kneeling and talking to the ancestral spririts.*
BOTTOM: *A powerful sangoma in a Shangaan village.*

BECOMING A WITCHDOCTOR:
"WHAT KICKS YOU, MASHUDU?"

Now we are back to where I began this story — with my convincing the witchdoctor I saw in the shop in Johannesburg to come home with me and my telling him I wanted to train as an *nyanga*. Once he had the approval to proceed, two other witchdoctors came to fetch me and took me off with them for my first real lessons.

We set out in my kombi, that useful vehicle I'd had for years, for going into the bush. I packed what I thought would be the right kind of clothes — wrap-around cotton African skirts and kaftans — presents, and food for the road. Nothing was said about making provision, but knowing that I was the one who was going to get the outing, I figured I was the provider — all the way. We went a couple of hundred miles north, leaving in the evening so they didn't lose that day's work, and over a week-end so they actually took off only two days. We got to a place out in the veldt and they said, "This'll do." We made a camp and lit a fire and ate our meal. We talked for a while, then I got into my sleeping bag. "I'm ever so sorry," I said. "This is wonderful, but as I'm doing all the driving I'm quite tired, so if you don't mind, good night." Then I noticed that one of them stayed awake all night, although we were absolutely safe. But one slept and one sat up, so they were watching over me all night. And never did they stop that care for the whole five days and nights. I felt so loved; it was a lovely, lovely experience.

We pushed on towards Venda. On the way, we went through Shangaan territory — towards the kraal of a Shangaan *sangoma*. I had met her before, but I didn't really know her, nor did she know me. And here I arrived at her *kraal* with an *nyanga* and a *mungoma!*

A group of seven acolytes was in training there. Acolytes join this profession and, if they can afford it, stay for three years and then graduate. If they cannot afford it, then they have Johannesburg jobs and they go to study for six months at a time. It is common in white society that people will come to me and say, "My cook says she's got to go home and bury her mother. But I know she buried her mother last November." I ask, "Is she taking six months off?" And if she is, it is probable that she is doing another portion of her training. There are many women, here in South Africa, who look sophisticated and Western, but who are fully trained in this profession. And you have to pay to learn. So it is also a question of whether you can afford to go there to study for three years.

The seven acolytes were one Venda man, one Tswana woman, one Xhosa woman, and four Venda women. Note the proportion of women to men. It is very significant. It struck me immediately that this seems to be a woman's profession. *Nyangas* — the herbalists — are, for the most part, men, but the *sangomas* — the really advanced psychic ones — are mostly women.

I was introduced to the *sangoma*, a woman whose English name is Nellie. Her surname is Mbara, and she is a very famous Shangaan *sangoma* in the north. This profession is completely non-tribal, in terms of who will go to whom. All over South Africa people will travel to the ones who are most famous at the time, no matter what their tribe. And as you see, even the class of acolytes was mixed Venda, Tswana, and Xhosa. It just happens that the Venda and Shangaan are leaders, because they live above the Tropic of Capricorn and have more *muti* up there. So people will come all the way from Cape Town to attend a ceremony or come for a cure.

Nellie was married to a very Westernised husband. And he wasn't stupid, either: When he bought her he bought a treasure house. He'd been working for the railways in Johannesburg but retired in his late thirties, no longer needing to work, as his clever *sangoma* wife kept him like a king. And yet still, in the tribal tradition, she asked his permission for everything. Every ceremony she would come and kneel at his feet in full regalia, whilst he sat in a chair in Western clothes. Only after obtaining his approval would she dance.

This first visit to her place was only for an introduction. She did not accept me, then — only much later, after I had been tested.

We then went on to the huts of my herbalist friend, Ndora Thiv-husiwi, and set off on the main purpose of this trip, with Ndora accompanying us the sixty kilometres to a valley called Mashau, to the home of the *nyanga*, Petros Nemaungani. Petros was a wise, middle-aged gentleman who had always been an *nyanga* and had three wives and twelve children. He had a circle of huts with one small rectangular hut alongside them. I had never met him before. He knew that an acolyte was coming for testing but he did not know that I was white. We smiled as we greeted each other; he did not show the surprise I am sure he felt.

We all went into one hut and each *nyanga* threw their bones, including Ndora. Each one had to decide whether or not I was acceptable. They didn't say much, but after some while all but Petros left. He and I stayed alone together, sitting on the mud floor of the hut. I felt some apprehension and excitement, as I was very keen to do this work, and I was worried that I would receive a No.

Petros has a round head sunk into thick shoulders and no hair at all — a shining bald head — but smiling, friendly eyes. He asked me, "What kicks you, Mashudu?" and I found that very difficult to answer. I did not really know what the motivation was, except a burning curiosity. He then threw the bones and started to describe me and my background, and it was all accurate: my English birth and — strange to me — my French family connections. I had not even known that my own mother was part French and that, in the south of France, I had had a great grandmother, but he saw and found all that. (Later on I checked this information and learnt it was so.)

Petros liked my vibes and said that my bridging and understanding of black cultures was a great asset and that this role was one I should fulfill: "It is right; it is good," he said. I was very happy indeed.

The others came back into the hut and we discussed how I would proceed. No one seemed to find it at all odd that this middle-aged, white, English-born woman wanted to know and learn all about their unique profession. I was made an immediate friend and to this day they are kind and good to me. Never once have I felt that I was an intrusion or not wanted. Quite the reverse.

I stayed in Venda five days and each day visited and worked with Petros at his place. He taught me to sit on the floor with no support — at first very difficult to do for hours at a time, as in the Western world we are used to chairs. "Do not think about the pain in your back; just concentrate on your work," he told me, and of course I can now sit for hours in that position. I asked him many questions and he was very tolerant of my lack of restraint. I wanted to know so much: How would I learn, when would the lessons start, who would teach me, where, and so on and so on.

It was decided that Ndora would take me out into the veldt and teach me about plants, whenever I could find time to take a visit up to Venda. I would go the the classes at Nellie Nyankwabe Mbara's whenever I could visit with her. And on a regular basis I would meet in Johannesburg with Nkhomelani Phineas Nekhavhambe, a well-known *nyanga* who lived permanently in the city. It was perfect.

That five-day visit was the turning point for me. Now that everyone had made the decision and, in particular, that someone as senior as Petros had given me his blessing, it all became possible. I left him with great joy and promised to return — and of course it was his place that later was chosen for the big ceremony when I was initiated.

We went back to see Nellie and my friends carefully explained to her what had happened. Her attitude towards me altered completely: I was made an instant member of the group of acolytes and included in the daily lessons. We all gathered in the special hut and sat on the mud floor, barefoot. (This is polite and expected of the acolytes and patients.) A small reed mat was placed on the floor in front of us, where the bones would be thrown, whilst Nellie, our teacher, sat on a stool behind us.

As a patient arrived at the opening of the hut, he would take off his shoes, leave them outside, step inside and shout out, "*Avum.*" We would reply, "*Savum.*" Again, "*Avum*" and from us, "*Savum.*" The patient would then sit down and shout out, "*Vhumani,*" and we would reply, all together, "*Siavuma.*" This, too, was repeated. This is a set ritual of behaviour: As there was no actual door to knock on, the words say, "Knock," and then "Come in" and "Welcome." It sets an important formality and tone and binds us all together in the performance.

Then the patient would tell us his name and the bag of bones would be handed to him, for him to breathe into deeply for a few minutes, to personalise the throw. As Nellie concentrated, she chanted phrases in Venda. All *nyangas* do this, all of them. The phrases are the Venda names for the patterns the bones have made as they fall, and the words for these patterns will be repeated over and over.

The names of the four dice also are called out and repeated as each one is identified, its position and message noted: *Limnana, Tshilaumi, Twalima, Lwhame*: male and female, young and old.

The diviner chants constantly, reading positions and patterns and what they imply. There are so many pieces and so many variations to learn, and in the beginning I reacted in a typically Western fashion — noting everything down on every case, as case histories are recorded in Western hospitals.

I was the eighth acolyte in the group, and they all became my friends. I was never actually told or instructed to do anything, but they expected that I would watch, copy, and join in, which is exactly what I did. I had my large black notebook always with me and I made copious notes, even sketching patterns in the fall of the bones and describing what the interpretation had been. I was the only one who did this, however; all the others seemed to just memorise everything. They didn't expect me to know the herbs and plants as they did, because they had grown up knowing quite a few and had lived with this custom and seen it in operation. For me, though, everything was strange and new — and, of course, very exciting.

At the end of the five days I returned to Johannesburg filled with stories, and after some short while my Wednesday lessons started with Phineas. They lasted for ten years. I got to know and love Phineas as a brother, and still today he is important in my life. He taught me not only the profession but humility and an understanding of man and our weaknesses and strengths. He showed how to live in service to one's people with one's gifts to give and not in exploitation. I am so grateful that I met him and that we have such a special relationship. No other white has become an initiated *nyanga* and Honorary Member of the Venda tribe.

KILLING THE WITCHDOCTOR'S COBRA

One day my teacher, Phineas Nekhavhambe, said to me, "You will kill a cobra for your task, this week." "No way," I told him. "I've done everything else, every test you've given me, but this is a No." I am not terrified, but I am certainly not happy around snakes. I will not kill a snake. "You are thinking white, again," he replied. He often criticised me on that ground. "It will be made possible for you to do it." And with that, away he went.

Phineas used to come to my Johannesburg home every Wednesday, to give me lessons. We would work together, then — before leaving — he would set me a task to do on my own. I had a special place set up for these lessons, with skins on the floor and all the artifacts of the trade ready. For years we did this together and had a very special relationship. He became like a big brother; we were in tune psychologically.

A little while after Phineas left, Cecil came home from business. "How's it, love? Had a good day? How was your lesson today?" "Oh," I said, "it was so exciting, but I have something to tell you, so come and sit down and have some tea." (When in doubt, always make tea!) "What's the matter?" he asked. "I have to go and kill a cobra." "ABSOLUTELY NO!" he said, just as I knew he would. He had never said No before — and I had done lots of funny things — but this time he said No; he was scared for me. I said, "Wait a minute. Phineas says it will be made possible for me to do it." "Oh did he?" said Cecil, immediately changing his attitude. "Well, then, where are you going to go? Where are there plenty of snakes?" "Botswana," I answered.

"Of course. Now, let's see. . . ." He had changed into a friend helping to organise my trip.

I left Cecil and packed up the kombi. "For how long are you going?" he asked. "I have to be back with the snake for next Wednesday's lesson, so it will be as many days as it takes to find one. It's gorgeous down there, so you don't expect me to just go and come back. I'll need a few days to stay and enjoy it." "OK", he said, "but I shall worry, you know. I wish there was a way you could let me know." "There is no way I can let you know. Once I'm there, that's it. But I'll be fine; you know that."

My husband trusted me, because he had watched me grow over a long period of time, but now he asked me to "throw the bones" to make sure it would all be OK. Cecil had learnt to believe the bones. They showed all to be well, so off I went. But I was worried. I loved my teacher, but I wondered if this wasn't going to be too big for me to handle. All the other tasks had been easy in comparison. After all, he didn't just say "a snake." He said, "a cobra." No choice. I don't like snakes. Not that I mind them at a distance, but close-to is another story. And to kill it you've got to get pretty close. I didn't take a gun (I never do).

All the tasks Phineas assigned I had to do on my own. It was like my training to be a nurse. I didn't mind; I loved those projects and handled most of them quite easily.

As I drove out along the bush track, not yet at Kudumalapapwe — the village where I wanted to stay — I sang to myself, as I always do when I am driving, a monologue of the day and the happenings, my thoughts, etc.: ". . . What a great day, but do I have a problem! Even if I find a snake what am I going to do? How on earth will I ever kill it? Oh, ho ho! What a big trouble I have here. Will I use a stick or whatever?" And you won't believe it, it's ridiculous, but at that precise moment a cobra came out of the the thicket in front of the kombi — at the right spot at the right moment — so that the wheels of the kombi went over it and killed it — just like that. In all my adult life that I've spent in the bush, never has a snake come out like that one, there — and it was not a ringhals, not a boomslang, not any of the other kinds of snakes found in that area. It was a cobra! The chances of my driving past that spot at that precise moment and having that snake there are amazing. A cobra — on the day that I needed it, in front of my kombi, at the right time. It was incredible. It was ridiculous. But it was true.

I jumped out and ran round the vehicle, shouting with joy, "THANK YOU VERY MUCH!" What a relief; what a pleasure! I danced and screamed out loud with my excitement, all alone in the bush, dancing in the sand like some nut, but what incredible knowledge it gave me. To accept the wisdom of my teacher, who had said, "It will be made possible for you." How could I possibly have ever doubted him? I never did again.

So there I was, not even right in the desert yet, on Day One, and my mission was accomplished. I couldn't believe it. I lit a fire immediately, found three large stones, put the kettle on, and made some tea. I just sat there looking at the snake, feeling incredible pleasure — like something you have longed for that is suddenly handed to you as a present.

Then I began to think: What was it Phineas told me to do, because when he told me of the task I didn't really listen to the details. I was too intent on my problems and the difficulty I imagined. All the time he was talking I was thinking to myself, This is crazy; I'm not going to do it; I'm not going to kill a cobra. . . . But if you had seen me when it happened, you wouldn't have recognised me. I was another person.

Now, I thought I recalled, he mentioned the brain. That's right, he wants me to bring back the snake's brain. He wanted to use it for special medicine, but it was also a project for me. There was a double purpose. But how to preserve the brain? I need a fire . . . well, all right, the fire is burning nicely . . . oh, yes, I've got to cut its head off and seal its neck in the hot ashes to burn it and seal it up, so that it will keep until I get back . . . because this is Day One and I have six more days before I see Phineas again. I'm not going to go back now, just because I've finished my project; no, now I'm going right in to have a holiday in the bush.

So I stayed there a long time, drinking tea, relaxing and working — cleaning up my cobra. When I tell this story to white friends, I can sometimes see in their reactions that they think I've gone completely off. This is why I've been apprehensive about this work, because there is more coming that will shatter some whites — understandably so — and if they don't meet me face-to-face, if they just read these stories, then they think I really am a nut.

In any case, I wrapped the snake in newspaper, stuck it away safely in the kombi, and pushed on into the desert. You must imagine that my aura, at that time, was positively electric — I was so very happy. I was driving up and down dirt dongas [ditches] and not worrying about the difficulties. Normally, you have to drive very carefully in such places, and concentrate, but that time I was driving by pure instinct — I wasn't really on this plane. I don't even remember the drive. But eventually I reached the destination village.

I jumped out of the kombi and greeted everyone with much laughter and smiles all round. They don't speak one word of English, and my Tswana was very limited, but we communicated our pleasure at seeing one another. I set up camp under a tree, and my old *nyanga* friend came over to see me. Having stayed there several times, I knew him quite well, although it is difficult to get very close to someone with whom you cannot talk and only speak in signs.

I sat there in front of him, he in a carved, wooden tribal chair, I on the ground, showing him my bag of bones and doing a reading, to show him that I knew how — and he fully accepted it.

I wanted him to see how far I had progressed. Having swept the sand with my hand and arm, to make a clean place to work, I threw the bones. I started a general reading, not for any particular person, but for local circumstances generally. They had had a terrible drought for years and years, and I "saw" rain coming in five months. I wanted so badly to tell them about it; I couldn't wait. "Please! please!" I shouted out, "Please find someone who can understand English. It's very important! I need to talk to you!" They didn't know what I said, but seeing my agitation they went off and found a girl about thirteen years old who had been to school and had enough English to understand. She sat down beside me and we started slowly — me reading the bones and she interpreting. It took a lot of time, but I was able to work. By this time, most of the village had come and sat round me — after, all, this was quite a happening.

I was reading really well. I was on a high of achievement, what with having killed the cobra and with the whole ambiance of the trip. One woman in the middle kept looking at me, and I could feel her longing. This often happens in a crowd, when one particular vibe draws you. I called her forward and started reading just for her. I found she had a real problem and slowly started to interpret it through the schoolgirl. This is what this profession is all about: finding the problem. When you are in tune, then it comes. It is a gift.

Suddenly I saw my *nyanga* friend get up and quietly leave. I thought to myself, "Oh, well, he is not satisfied and doesn't think I'm any good." But I went on and just did my best. The people were happy to listen — it was like someone coming down in a spaceship and entertaining the whole village, something that would never happen again, because whites in my profession are very few (to say nothing of a white *woman!*)

Then my friend came back and sat down again. I had more or less finished and was packing up my things when he put out his hand and said, "Mashudu, Mashudu. You are ready." And he opened his hand and placed into mine a bone from the antbear — a fairly large nocturnal animal, like a bear with a long snout. This bone, plus the one from a springbok, you never get yourself. All the others you have to find, but these two must be given to you when you are deemed ready, not by your own teacher but by another member of the profession who makes the decision. Through all the years, I had been asking Phineas, "When will I be ready? When will I get my important bones? When will I get my antbear?" "When you are ready," he said, "it will happen. Not before." You have to be patient — difficult for whites. Phineas spoke to me with gentle control, as if to a child. My nyanga friend appreciated my level of expertise and saw and felt my knowledge, and he wanted to be the one to give the honour. He could see in my bag of bones that it had not happened yet. He could see that I had done certain things but had not yet achieved that bone. That bone says much — it is like a graduation bone. It says that I have reached a high level. It speaks to people who see me throw; the bone tells them I am not a junior.

The tribe saw him bestow this on me and were impressed. So in that village I will always have a special place. I need never take a thing to eat; I could always arrive, live there and be welcomed as part of the community. It was a very special act indeed — the giving of an honour and the acceptance of it on an equal footing. Friendship made public. An acceptance by the whole for an individual.

When I saw that antbear bone in my hand I was very moved. It is a day I shall never forget.

When I arrived home and told Cecil the news, he was as happy for me as if I had just achieved an academic degree. On Wednesday my teacher came, as always. Tribal tradition says you place gifts in the bag, so I had wrapped the cobra in gift wrap, with nice paper and ribbon, and placed it in my bag of bones. We took off our shoes (a sign of respect) and sat on the floor. As I threw my bag, out came the package, which I presented to him. He immediately spotted the antbear bone and said to me, "Oh, now we are ready." I said, "Yes, I will tell you about that, but first my present." I couldn't wait to show him the cobra head, but he simply placed it to one side. I was so disappointed. "*Say* something. *Please* say something. Ask me if I did it," I implored. "I told you that you would do it. I know that you did it. I do not need to ask you," he replied quietly. And we went on with the lesson.

THE BONES

t is difficult to explain how one "reads" the bones. It is a gift. But I can give you some examples.

One day I was sitting in QwaQwa, in the mountains. I actually went down there on a political assignment, but I always pack my bones, because who knows? I was in a village with some very poor people and met a very nice old couple in one of the huts. As we spoke and got to know each other, it seemed right to "throw" for them. As I began, I said, "Oh, my friend, that foot; it is in many pieces, that foot." Once I start I don't look at him. People say to me, "But you're a nurse; you're looking at a diagnosis professionally," but I'm not. I don't even look at the faces. I am unaware even of who is sitting there, I am concentrating so deeply. I asked the old man to tell me about it, and he explained that he had been working on the docks, unloading ships, and one day a crane broke and a whole crate fell on his foot and crushed it into lots of little pieces. It had been fixed up, but the bits were still in there! He had shoes on, and I had never met him before, but I could read his problem in the bones.

Once I found his broken foot, the whole village came and said, "Tell us when it will rain." If I can find the rain I tell it, but if I can't, I say I don't know. You must always tell the truth; you don't play fairy tales and build someone up falsely. If you see death, you never tell death, and you never tell the diseases of death. There are positives and negatives in every interpretation.

I never accept payment for what I do. It is a service. But people often want to do something, in thanks. One woman whom I touched with my work did something very special indeed for me. My teacher had said I needed a fire symbol for my bag. I wasn't going to put a matchstick in there, and I tried to think what was strong and has a great message that says 'fire.' Two years went by and still I did not have my fire symbol.

One day a package arrived — a matchbox with a cowrie shell inside which you could see had been burnt in a fire. The accompanying note — from a woman at a university who had heard about me from a mutual friend — said, "I am an archaeologist and I go on digs, and I was down in the Cape Province with my team and my professor and we discovered Bushman ruins. There was a very old midden from a fire, with all sorts of things which we put in bags to bring back to the university to study. There were hundreds of these shells, from the fire." The site was about 3000 years old. She had asked her professor if she might take one of the burnt cowries, and he thought she wanted a remembrance of the dig. "No, I don't," she said, "but there is a lady in Johannesburg who very badly needs a powerful fire symbol, and I interpret this as being that kind of . . ." "Oh, how interesting," he interrupted. "Yes, certainly you may take one." Can you image how I felt when I opened that package? Here was something that came out of Bushman hands, the Bushmen who were so important to me. I was so grateful. To everyone else it may be just a bit of old broken shell, but to me it was very special.

Another time, in Johannesburg, a good friend phoned to say she had friends visiting from Scotland who wanted "a real African experience" and could she bring them over and would I throw the bones for them? I don't do this sort of thing for fun and amusement, but I told her to bring them round for tea. We had a very nice conversation. They were charming people, really, with a lovely young son, so I threw for them and did a reading. They were not on the floor, they did not take their shoes off. They were overseas tourists and I did not put them through all that kind of trouble, because I thought it was going to be a very superficial reading. I described their house and some water damage to one side of it, and when they denied it told them just to mark down the date and check it out. (I later learnt their water geyser on that end of the house had, in fact, burst just prior to the day we met.) Then I did their health, which was fine, and a few other things I thought were of interest.

I finished the reading and the mother and father were most appreciative and leant over and said, "Oh we wish we could do something for you. You have made us such a wonderful morning. What else do you need? You did mention the kit wasn't full, yet." So I said, "Well, I need one more piece, a stone of some kind, to relate to the South African soil. There is a mountain in the Cape that is one of the rare places in the world where asbestos was oxygenised in the long-ago geological strata, and in parts of that mountain it's deep gold and black and brown, and in others it's rust and the stone is magnificent. I need a rough piece. I can't have anything that's been tumbled for jewellery. I'd love a piece of this 'tiger's eye' as we call it."

The young boy stepped forward, put his hand in his pocket, and pulled out a piece of rough, raw tiger's eye. "Auntie," he said to me, "I want you to have this. I climbed the mountains last week, with my parents, and we found it there. "Tiger" is my nickname at home, when I play soccer, so it was very special to me when I saw it, but I don't want it anymore. I want you to have it. I want it to be in your care. I want you to think of me when you see it in your bag." He put it down on the floor next to me, and I cried. This little red-haired boy and the red stone. I was very much moved.

Phineas, when I told him the story, said, "It was meant to be. Things happen in life that are meant to happen. It's not an accident at all." Whites would say, "What an incredible coincidence," but he would say, "No, it's not a coincidence."

So, those two items in my bag — the cowrie shell and the piece of tiger's eye — are very precious indeed.

Some of the bones and other items in a witchdoctor's kit may be purchased. In fact, there are special places that sell those things. Many must be in pairs, male and female, because you've got to have every single nuance of patterns of behaviour — strong and weak, male and female, black and white, fast and slow. The crocodile bones are called the lions, because they are so wily and so strong. You must know that in my tribe the crocodile is very significant, as it is a very wily and a very clever animal. It is the only animal we've got left that relates to the prehistoric times. That animal and the cycad plants. (The cycads are so rare they are listed, in our country. It is illegal to collect them from the veldt.)

Everything I obtained was always placed immediately into the skin bag and the next Wednesday, when Phineas came to my house for my lesson, I would throw the bones first, to show him my learning of that week, then he would throw his bones and teach me lessons with his. I had only one week to do or find whatever he instructed.

One week I had to find the shells that determine sex — one male and one female, completely different types of shells. The tiger cowrie is for women. It is very large and personifies the womb. Its shape is like a large womb. There is a certain conch shell for men (the penis), a small ringed cowrie shell for the baby girl, and a spotted cowrie for the baby boy. I obtained the last three immediately, from a young twelve-year-old girl who wanted me to have shells from her collection, but I didn't have the large tiger cowrie for women; that only came into my life much later, when another friend brought it back to me from a holiday in Durban. Things come, I learnt, if you have patience. So now I have the full kit of shells, all of good colours and quality. Months would go by, each week practising — as in piano, constant practise, learning by experience — and then Phineas would set another task. There was no set pattern of work; as and when he decided I was ready to do another step, he gave it to me.

One day he said, "Now you need money, to show wealth or lack of it." "Right," I replied, and I had one week to decide what coins would play a significant role for me in the kit. I was already thinking about it whilst he was sitting there telling me of my new task. He always had tea with me before he left, sitting there just enjoying each other's company. I was forty-nine, then, and he was about forty, and each week we spent together, as he trained me, our bond grew stronger. I had a nice coin collection from all over the world — not large, but interesting. I am not a knowledgeable coin collector; I collected the coins that attracted me for what they were, what was on them, and where they came from. For this new task I didn't have to go out looking; I just took out my own collection and decided what I would add to my kit, thinking to myself, "male, female, age, youth, power."

The first coin I chose was an eight-sided coin from England, with the Queen pictured on it. The value of the coin was not relevant, but an eight-sided coin is unusual — not like normal money; a special coin. Then I chose a round coin from Swaziland, with an edge like a flower, curved in small half-rounds all round the coin — also not a normal round coin, but special, and with the King of Swaziland on it. So there I had it: male, female, black, white, a king and a queen for power. I added a small silver sixpence from England, for the lower-income decisions: You can't read on the big ones if a child wants to know about an increase in pocket money or a similar simple request. You must have small money as well. I already had realised this, by observing Phineas' bag.

I put all these coins in my bag and the next Wednesday I threw and watched Phineas looking. He looked at my money, turning them over and working out why I chose each coin. "Very powerful money," he said, "Very good thinking; not white thinking." So I think that I am getting there, in spirit.

The next week he brought a piece of gum and a root. Sometimes he brought medicines — natural ones, from plants — for me to chew to help me, but this day he said, "Now you are going to make your bones strong for you, and you have to treat them." He took my coins and placed them on the floor, then took the gum, into which he had worked the root, and rolled it into tiny little sausages and placed one on each coin in an upright position. He placed the coins in circles, right close, with the ones I wasn't reading well in the center and the stronger ones on the outside. (The ones you are confident with and reading well need the least attention.) Everything is laid out in circles in the order that you want them strengthened in power. He lit the gum (a kind of incense) and it burnt with a fragrant smoke. You must stay with it, lean over it, talk to it, breathe in the smoke, concentrate on the bones and what you do with them, until the gum is burnt to ashes. This ceremony will make the bones stronger. You must do this every day for a week, changing the pattern of the pieces — bones, shells, and coins — until they have all been thoroughly treated.

Every Wednesday, when my husband came home from work, he knew that I had been in a training session with Phineas. Setting down his briefcase, he always asked, "How did your lesson go today?" and I always replied with some details of the day's lesson. But on the day I learnt about treating the bones I could not answer him: I was concentrating on the smoke, the bones, and the strengthening of my kit. He walked over to me, leant over, and asked, "What on earth is happening here?" I said only, "I am making my bones strong," so he went away and left me until the treatment was finished. I did this night after night for a whole week. What Phineas was doing, at this point, was instilling ritualistic patterns into my Western home, to introduce me and Cecil to it and to make us grow. We both were beginning to see that this was not like anything else in our experience — and indeed it is not!

The next week Phineas brought me another root, quite a big piece, and he told me, "Now you will see how your first stick is to be used." At my very first lesson he had said I would need a porridge stick with four prongs, made from a tree — a new one, never used. It happened that I had one, in my collection of African artifacts, and when I brought it out for him he had said, "It was meant to be; it was meant to be." Then he said, "Take a small bowl and put it in your bathroom. Place your four wooden dice in it and every night shave some of this root into the bowl, with some water, and whip it up with the porridge stick." It is just like detergent and makes lots of froth and foam. He then told me, "You must wash with the foamy water and you must leave the dice in that water all night and wash again in it in the morning. The dice will get strong in that *muti* water." So that bowl stayed in my bathroom and I followed Phineas' instructions every morning and every night for a week. And every night my husband would come in to wash and clean his teeth, as I was busy whisking away with my special bowl, and one day he said, "My, living with a witch is certainly different." But he didn't mind and was always tolerant of all my doings. [In a magazine interview some years hence, Cecil Graham was quoted as saying that "living with Rae you don't need television!"]

Another day, Phineas said to me, "Now you will go and get the bones you need for wisdom and strength. You will need two crocodile bones and two baboon bones — male and female for each." I looked up at him in disbelief. "Where on earth am I going to get bones from those animals? I live in Johannesburg, Phineas!" "You will find them," he said, and away he went for another week. Each week he gave me these tasks that really tried my ingenuity. On this occasion I thought to myself, "The blighter — every week he gives me these tasks and then goes comfortably home, leaving me in a mess." I sat down and thought about it, knowing there was no way I was going out into the bush to trap animals but unable to think of a way to get them.

Making enquiries through my black friends, I discovered there was a witchdoctors' market place, in Johannesburg, called the MaiMai. It was very exclusive and difficult to get into, with a high wall around it. No white people went there. I had never heard of it before but now, in my need, I discovered its existence. It had a guard at the entrance gate and at that time was controlled by the government authorities. I realised that that was where all the witchdoctors went. After all, they could not always be hoofing off into the bush for the plants, skins, and bones they needed. This unique facility was controlled and guarded by the government because it was on government land and because witchdoctors had complete freedom of movement at a time when no other blacks did. Even then the government realised that witchdoctors had a major role to play and fulfilled a definite need. The MaiMai market was constructed not for their protection but to place them all together in a suitable environment, rather than have them all over the city. They didn't need protection; no-one would have dared touch them.

So I went to the MaiMai with some Venda friends, having first gone to the authorities in town to get a permit to enter the market. I had asked to see one of the senior commissioners, to ask for this unusual request — a permit to go into a black marketplace where white women just never went. I dressed soberly, in a skirt and blouse, and tried to look as responsible as possible. Sitting at his desk, I made my request: "I need to go into the MaiMai." "Oh, you're such a nice lady but no, madam, I don't think it would be nice for you to go in there." "Well," I said, "I've got my gardener to look after me, and I'm as nervous as you are but I have to go." "Oh, you are probably writing a book," he replied, and gave me my permit! Then he asked, "How long do you think I should let you in there for?" "One hour would be fine," I responded calmly. "No, no madam. If you are doing some work that is essential for you I will give you three hours, but do take care, and don't go in alone!" "Fine," I told him, inwardly grinning with delight.

We got to the gate and the black policeman couldn't believe that I had a permit. He expressed surprise but opened the gate and let me in. The building was filled with rows of little shelters, wooden for the most part, with tin roofs. Each had a counter, in front of which were the grinding stones, with people sitting and working, preparing *muti*. Displayed all over were leopard and baboon skins, lions' paws, stones, rocks and bones of every kind, heaps of herbs, shelves of roots — counter after counter — and behind each, a person from every different tribe. These were not *nyangas* or *sangomas* but wholesalers, there to sell whatever the witchdoctors needed. I know the facial characteristics of each tribe, so as I walked down the little alleyways between shelters I greeted everyone, each in his own language: Tswana, Shangaan, Xhosa, Zulu, Venda. I wanted them to know that I knew who was from which tribe and could greet each one correctly, without being told who was what. There must have been about fifty or sixty counters. I was looking for someone from Venda and, when I found her, I smiled and said, "Hello, how are you? I'm from Venda, too."

She invited me inside, where there was a small place in the shelter where we could sit down and talk. I did not behave in the typical white way — by saying I'd come for this and that and quickly doing my business — but, rather, took the time to chat first, and got to know her. She was young and very pretty and shyly asked my companion about me. "Who is this woman?" she wanted to know. "She is an *nyanga*; she is an acolyte in training." "OOOOH Really!" She spoke five or six languages, as most Vendas do. They learn all the other languages, although the other tribes do not speak Venda, for the most part. All the people around were shouting out, *"Who is she? Who is she?"* And they were hearing and being told, so in no time at all the whole lot knew who I was and what I was. The whole MaiMai knew. It cannot be very often that a white visited there, and certainly not a witchdoctor in training, so they were coming round corners and peeking and watching me the whole time I was there. It was quite an experience!

I bought my two baboon bones and my two crocodile bones, taking about an hour to choose them, all of us laughing and enjoying the experience. When I had finished, the young Venda woman put into my hand a springbok bone — the other one (besides the antbear bone) which I could not buy. It must be given, by someone in the profession who believes I am now strong enough to have it. I had taken my bag with me and by this stage had thrown it out, to show her just where I was in training, and so was touched and pleased by her assessment of me. The springbok bone indicates speed and cleverness.

She also could tell my level by the stick I was carrying: The first stick, which one uses for six months, is the wooden porridge stick; then a wooden stick covered with small glass beads, then the tail of a cow, then the tail of a horse. At that time I was up to the tail of a horse and there is only one more tail to go — the tail of a wild animal. I have one waiting already, if I ever reach that far.

My wild animal tail is from a wildebeest which the Bushmen hunted and killed one day when I was with them. I didn't want to spoil the skin for them in any way and so asked for the tail, which they were pleased to give to me.

As I needed each stick and Phineas told me which one to get, I discovered often that I already had it in my collection of artifacts. But I did not have the tail of a cow; it just never had occurred to me to collect one. And we used to own cows, in Venda. I wished I'd taken one from one of those.

When I told Phineas I was lacking there, he said with quiet conviction, "Don't worry; it will come." That evening I told Cecil my story. Shortly thereafter, Cecil made a business trip to what was then Rhodesia (now Zimbabwe) and returned with a gift for me, suitably wrapped with ribbons. It was a most beautiful tail of a cow, with a carved handle, that he had purchased up there in a market place. The other businessmen were buying boxes of chocolates and soap for their wives, but Cecil knew what would please me most. Imagine the reactions of the other men, when he said he'd bought his wife a cow's tail!

My horse's tail also has a story associated with it. We went camping at Victoria Falls, many years ago, with Clive and Felicity, who were seven and six years old. When Felicity fell and almost drowned in a crocodile-infested river, I could no longer bear the sound of the roar of the river at night, and we moved inland near a large black village. There I saw the tail of a horse with the hair fixed into a handle of horn, carved in the shape of an elephant head. As my tribal chief was Thoyandou, "the head of an elephant," this stick was a tribal totem for me and I bartered a very good cooking pot to get it. That was years before I ever dreamt of becoming a witchdoctor, so when Phineas saw it he was speechless.

My throwing bag, too, is made from a skin I already had collected. It is tied with a piece of goatskin found in a *kraal* in Botswana.

When you throw the bag you give it to the patient to hold and breathe deeply into, to personalise the throw. Then you take it back and shake it several times, banging it on the floor once or twice before emptying it (throwing the pieces) onto a special reed mat, on the floor. You then take your stick in your hands, twirling it a little as you concentrate and start to analyse the patterns of the bones and dice.

We look first at the four wooden divining dice, which have a carved side and a plain side, a head end and a feet end. *Limnana* is the young woman; *Twalima* is the old woman; *Tshilaumi* is the young man; *Luhame* is the old man. These four are the basis of the whole profession; you can work with just those. I've seen *nyangas* in the desert, where resources are few, with four like these but not carved in wood because there are no big trees. They make them out of horn, beautifully carved and marked.

For six months you work and learn these. They are the basic family. Then comes the extended family, so you have to have a similar set made of something else. Then you go to the furthest extended family, and that is when you get the four ivory discs — usually given to you by your teacher or a family connection. Mine are fairly new, not beautifully worn like Phineas'. He inherited his from his grandfather, so they are very old and have been much used. Sometimes I need all of these, as my family is twenty-three people. Not that you need a piece for every member, but enough to identify group behaviour and circumstances. Individuals will be singled out for specific readings, if necessary.

There is a special medium-sized shell, a conch with a frilled edge, called the house of Amalozi (the house of the spirits), which is used in describing a person's house and the side of the entrance. A small white river pebble shows where the water source (the bathroom) is, and another one shows where the fire (kitchen) is. Most of the time the bones are right; you just have to learn to read them correctly. I cannot tell you why the patterns fall so accurately. That I cannot explain, and no one ever has described it to me. All I know is that most of the time the message is fully accurate, unless the reader is weak, out of practise, or never properly learnt the profession.

A small shell from the ocean tells me about overseas journeys; another of banded agate is used to show the land.

Phineas told me to find two baboon bones because these animals are the closest in patterns of behaviour to human beings. They show the relationship between husband and wife, everything about a marriage.

It is essential for the diviner to work slowly though the process. You may describe the house and then find the problem is with the husband or wife, or one of the children, or with workmates. At that point, having identified the person giving the problem, you ask for the name and throw the bones again on that name. You may throw them all again or only certain ones you feel are needed. You throw all of them in the beginning, but during the long process of a full reading you may pick certain groups and throw them separately, again and again, until the picture emerges. You cannot just answer one question right away.

I added shells to my bag after many years, when I discovered that certain tribes need certain emphasis. Particular shells are for the Pondo people — for them they are holy shells. They come in along their coastline, way to the south and east. I would need those shells only very seldom, for those black tribes.

A black of any tribe will relate to a kit. Mine is a very powerful kit, as there is hardly anything missing: some things, but not many.

You have to have two bones from pigs, because a pig is an animal that mucks round in the dirt and snuffles like the antbear. It is an animal very close to black life because you can keep a pig in a tiny enclosure and feed it with offal and rubbish and it doesn't cost you any money. So it is very powerful in their lives. You must also have nine goat bones. I have eight, so I've still one more goat to go. I may never do that — but it just depends: If I'm in a black village and somebody kills a goat, I'll go and barter for it. It must be one bone from each goat — you can't just take four knuckles from one goat. That's why they're all different sizes.

There is one bone that is not 'clean' because the bone of the goat that I kill must remain unwashed, and this represents my goat. This says to everybody who sits here who is black, "She's done her goat ceremony."

Certain bones relate to disease — some bones for illnesses above the waist and others for below. Others represent people — male and female, young and old. Some of them seem to have "eyes" which, depending on their position when they fall, indicate a variety of things and give me very specific information. The white stone, which indicates death, came from a very special burial place: Avebury, in England.

When you're reading the bones for a patient, for any particular problem, and you've already discovered whether the problem is financial, psychological, or physical, you look at whether there is another witchdoctor, another *nyanga* in this area, who may or may not be supportive of what you are doing. In other words, you are looking for the patient's "threat" person, in the immediate territory. Then you ascertain whether there is a positive or a negative vibe from that area. Finding the *nyanga* in that area can have a very vital bearing on what you're doing with this patient, whether or not the patient has been to see that other *nyanga*. You may have to see the patient again and again, and the attitude and influence of another *nyanga* could be of value in your work.

The antbear bone, in the kit, is the one you look at to discover the whereabouts of the doctor in that area. When I am in homeland areas, in a primitive village, it is very important that I discover where that *nyanga* — or *mungoma* or *sangoma* — is. I always say to the assembled group, "I wish to go and pay respects to that *nyanga;* will you take me there?" and I will pay him a visit. First of all, it is polite, but it will also be of great value that rather than have him against your work he will be supportive of it.

When you do a psychological reading for a person in the Western style, you give psychological tests and, after three months or so, reach a conclusion as to where the patient has been and where he is now, in his development and problems. That can all be done within an hour, in a reading of the bones. A psychologist from Wits University once watched my teacher and me and said, "It's amazing how quickly you've arrived at the same decisions we have." It used to be that doctors saw a patient, diagnosed him, and offered treatment. Now it is acknowledged that the patient is a part of a much larger group and the influences are important, physically and psychologically. If you accept that you can get a headache because of a problem, and not because there is something wrong with your head, then you'll understand fully what I mean. Today, when a senior executive goes for an interview with a company, they want to meet his wife and they want to know his relationship with her. The blacks have known that for centuries; it's just an accepted fact that as an individual you are not an individual alone. You are part of a much larger sphere, and that sphere has its power over you — *for* you or *against* you. It is important to know what that power is. And that's what *nyangas* discover.

Sometimes, when I could see real health problems, I would say "Now I will tell you what we are going to do," and I would take them straight-away to my doctor, whose rooms [office] are quite close by.

My doctor (white, medical) and I had a very close relationship. The day I "graduated" and became a witchdoctor he sent me a cable which said, "Welcome to the profession. You are now a doctor." He is the only medical doctor who has acknowledged me. There are those who accept what I do, but he welcomed me to the profession as an equal.

When we arrived at his rooms, his nurses — who knew me well by then — took us right in. When the doctor came in to see us, I would take his hand to the patient and we three would hold hands together, and I would say, "I am now giving my power through this doctor to you because I am not reading well today and I cannot help you, but this man can help you, for me." The doctor knew that if I brought him someone, I had detected something serious that needed Western medical care.

On the other hand, when the doctor had a patient who had had all the tests and all the x-rays and still he could not find anything wrong with him, he sent his patients to me, saying, "I know just the lady who can help you." And it worked! I got psychologically broken people that we knew we must build up.

Nyangas are basically herbalists and diagnosticians. We are psychologists. We're shrinkheads, but not at the highest level. I don't know the exact percentage, but I would guess we can cope with about 70% of everything out there. Sometimes, for the cases the doctor sends to me, we go to a *mungoma* — a "specialist" witchdoctor, very psychic, very spiritual. *Nyangas* and *mungomas* both divine with a bag of bones and analyse the problem. Both are diagnosticians. Other witchdoctors, *sangomas*, do not work with bones but go into trancelike states and talk with strange voices. They wear the red and blue skirts that all the rest of us wear, but they also have a third skirt — the lowest of the three — which is black. Their profession is one far more spiritual, as when they talk to their ancestral family spirits and get messages from them. They do face-to-face individual problems but also the larger community problems, and in the old days each chief had his own consultation *sangoma* for advice.

I am often misrepresented in newspapers as being a *sangoma*, but I am not and do not wish to be at all. These are the people who used to "smell out" and call for a sacrifice to the spirits. In the minds of people who do not know, this is what a witchdoctor is — someone always evil, always savage and primitive. This is a broad, uneducated assumption. There were many who did wrong and certainly did kill, but there are many also who perform a service as psychologist or psychiatrist. They have great ceremonies where the drums play and there is much dancing, in full regalia — beads and feathers — and it is very colourful and exciting. Of course one can become easily hypnotised and fall in a faint, in these circumstances.

I have never seen anyone "smelt out" (because, of course, the law now forbids such things), but in the past, the person to whom the *sangoma* pointed became a zombi immediately and had to be supported on each side or they would fall down. It was said that this person contained the spirit that was doing damage to the village — no rain, no crops, cattle dying, the illness of the chief, or whatever — and it was necessary to appease these spirits with a sacrifice. The horn of an animal, either a buck or a cow was inserted into their side and turned and turned, to make an exit for the spirit to come out.

Obviously this doesn't take place anymore, but there is an element in this level of the profession that is not my cup of tea. I know seventeen *sangomas,* some of them as close friends and some only as acquaintances, and I am allowed to be present at their ceremonies, but always alone, no other whites with me. I have participated only in the social part of their lives; I have not done an intimate study of them.

Usually the *sangomas* are working with a powerful force, whilst we the *nyangas* are more like GP's, or general practitioners, on a different level entirely. But we are all psychologists, and with many people here still in the transition from the Third World to the First, with all the accompanying pressures, the role of the witchdoctor is more important, not less. Herbalists, *nyangas, mungomas,* and *sangomas* are growing in number and are to be found everywhere, in the towns and cities, in the country, everywhere. And they are always available. There are also wizards, called *valoi,* who, like the *sangomas,* have great psychic powers.

Blacks understand the psychology of illness. When advising a patient they evaluate the problem, give it a name, then start building up the patient in such a way that they find the ability to cope, to find the inner strength to overcome it.

Once and once only I worked for someone *in absentia.* I had divined for two elderly whites here in Johannesburg and they remembered me, so when a friend of theirs in Cape Town was in great trouble they phoned me. They were elderly and had to make a big decision nearly at the end of their lives, and they needed someone to clarify things. I recognised their voices over the phone, but when one of them asked me to help this lady I said I couldn't do it, that I'd never done it before. "Please, please," he said. "We don't know where else to go."

It was a bit sticky. How could I get a vibe over the phone? In the past I had sometimes brought home a piece of someone's hair and placed it inside the bag of bones to personify the throw, but then I had met the person and felt a vibe. In this case I had not met or even spoken to the woman.

I thought about it and said, "All right, I'll tell you what I'll do. Tonight at 8:00 PM you sit with her and hold her hands, because I have held your hands and that will be a bond. Whilst you hold hands, think about me. I will sit on the floor of my bedroom, quietly alone, and do a reading." And so I did. I took a pencil and paper and wrote down everything that I saw. The next morning I phoned Cape Town and read it out. It was all accurate, which meant I could give advice, knowing I was on the right vibe with her. At 1000 miles' distance. It's incredible, but it gives me such pleasure to be able to help people. So I threw for them and discovered exactly what it was and gave them advice. That's the only one I have ever done without a face-to-face relationship, and I only tried because her problem was very bad.

When I went to Israel and made many friends I threw for absolute strangers who asked me. I was in an apartment, once, at a party, and the folks in the flat next door came in and said they had a problem and would I advise. All the Israelis in the room wanted to see me work, and this was a way for them to see. I asked where North was, as I couldn't see for myself. In the southern hemisphere, North and East are positive because the sun is strong in those two positions. West and South are negative. In the northern hemisphere it is the opposite. So I must know which way I am facing before I can read the bones.

Immediately I started reading I found death, in a child. Now, what to do? They were all looking at me. I said, "There is something very unhappy, here. I don't quite know how to tell you." They said, "We know what you have found. It has just happened." So then I could tell them that I had found a small little girl who had just died. "Yes," they said. They wanted help in their agony, which I tried to give.

DIVINING

The first patient I got (this was in 1975, the same year I began studying with Phineas) was from Alexandra township. She was a young girl who couldn't walk, and the doctors in the clinic knew there was nothing wrong with her. They had done every test in the book. The doctor, there, phoned me up and said, "This is the most difficult thing I've ever done, but I'm asking you for help with this particular patient." I said, "I'm sure we can help her; bring her over to my house." So this white lady doctor and one of her helpers, a student, arrived with the black girl — a young woman, actually, of about twenty or twenty-five — and carried her in and put her on the floor, where we worked. Phineas wasn't here; he was out of town, so I was all alone.

I started throwing the bones and could see there was nothing wrong with her. So I looked at her and said, "My girl, you must have had a very bad experience." And then I threw the bones on that, looking for some pattern of behaviour, some element that was destroying her. I found her near water, and I said, "Oh, you went down to the stream, in Alex," and she said, "Yes." And then I found a snake, a python in the river bed that had said to her, "You have been naughty," or "You have done something wrong and you'll never walk again." And so she couldn't walk, because the snake had said she couldn't walk. This must have been a dream, when she was "possessed" for a few minutes. So, now that I found out the problem, all I had to do was to convince her that my spirit was stronger than the snake's.

It was a bitter cold day, and I had put on some weight, so my winter coat would no longer button up — which meant I was being told to find someone to give it to. A beautiful coat. And I looked at her and thought, "She is my size." So, first of all, I won her over, and then I said to her, "You can walk, and I'm going to make it possible for you to walk. Just let me go away for a minute." And I went away and fetched the coat. And I walked across the room and looked at the young girl and said to her, "It's yours, if you come and fetch it." And she just got up and walked to me and put the coat on.

The doctor was amazed, but of course she told everyone about it, and so Phineas and I started getting lots and lots of phone calls. Once we had a woman come to us for *muti* to use to kill her husband! Of course we refused. Another time, a young man came to me, in distress, saying that his girlfriend was very beautiful and very tall and could I please make him taller. We could have made him feel taller psychologically, but there were so many other people in real need that we turned him away with just a little encouragement. I had a priest friend, who used to help all sorts of people, come to me once saying he couldn't talk to anyone else. He was a monk, but he was very much in love with a woman and was in a real dilemma: If he married her he would have to give it all up, and did he love her that much? It took me many days with him to sort it all out, but I got a "Yes" and he married her. They have a wonderful marriage and continue to do good things. The woman was a missionary worker. They must have talked about it, in the church, because pretty soon I had four nuns come to me — not Catholics, but they came to me through the church. I really didn't want to get involved with this, but they begged me and so I agreed. It turned out to be a political problem — nothing to do with their faith — so it worked out easily.

It is sometimes difficult for men to come, especially to talk about business, because to them it shows weakness. But they cannot discuss what's bothering them with their associates, so they come to me. They know it will all be private and confidential, so they can pour it all out and find a solution.

One day an executive from a big company phoned me. They were in the middle of a big deal with a French company, but the French representative was nervous about signing the contract. The South African said to me, "We're not asking you to tell him we're a good company, but will you see this man?" and I agreed. A big, chauffeur-driven car arrived with the man, whom I welcomed to my home and we sat down on the floor on the skins. I explained that, as a sign of respect, he must take off his shoes and showed him where to sit. "On the floor?" he asked. "Yes," that is how we work." An elegant man, he was.

"First," I explained to him, "I'm going to describe you and your background and everything about you, and then I'll come to the business, but I have to do it from scratch." I said, straightaway,

"You live near water; it must be a river, and you're not in a house, you're in a very tall building. Do you live in a block of flats [apartment building] overlooking the Seine, in Paris?" And he said Yes. And then I said, "You have a wife and a daughter, and the daughter's going to get married soon." Then it started. I said, "But she doesn't like the man she is going to marry! You want her to marry him, but she doesn't want to. It's probably to do with your company, then. She hates him! She's distraught! Why are you pushing her?" And then he got interested. "Now," I said, "let me look at you deeper. The relationship with your wife, it's awful. You never let her make up her mind about anything! You dominate these two women in your apartment. They are just there for you. You order them around about everything. I don't think you should make your daughter get married. I think, when you get back, you must cancel all the arrangements and then wait and see. If it's meant to be, she'll come back to you and say yes, she does love him, but don't push this wedding. And your wife, from now on you allow her to become a human being." I was reading really very well, by this time. You know, I had a French great-grandmother; maybe she was pushing all this down to me. And then I said, "If you could just come to terms with yourself you would have a much happier life and your indecisions would fall away, because you wouldn't always be pushing and pushing people. I would imagine that if you do that to your lovely wife you do that to everyone around you in your company as well. Let's have a look at that." I said, "The product is one that is very successful. The company here is going to give you all the support you are worried about; it's going to be successful and I have no difficulty whatsoever with your signing that contract. It's fine and it's good. But I have great difficulty with your pattern of human relationships and your life at home, and that's all I'm going to say to you."

He sat back and said, "Dear God, I *am* pushing my daughter to get married and I didn't realise how bad it was. My God, my God. I will not make her get married." "And your wife?" I said. "Why don't you show her you love her? Let her make a few decisions on her own. Do you realise what those two will do for you if you go back a changed man?" I will never know what he did when he went home, but he did sign the contract and it was a very successful venture. I don't know how much I helped, but the next day the chauffeur arrived from the company with a great big bowl of flowers. You see, they know I will not take payment for this. Phineas says I must not take money; I will lose my gift. I don't need to make my living at it. It is a gift that has been given, so I've never made a ha'penny from it. But I do get wooden or bone crocodiles and other lovely things — often flowers, because they know I love Nature.

One day, at a reception, a mayor came over to me and put his hand on mine and said, "I must talk to you." "*You*, Mr Mayor?" I asked. You see, you never know who is having problems. The next day, he came over. He was concerned about someone very close to his family. "They'll never come to see you," he told me. "They don't have the courage to call you, but please do me a favour." I said I'd go to them and next day I phoned the people. The wife answered.

"I understand you have a problem," I told her, "and I'm coming out, right now." And I got in my car and drove over there — quite a long way. When I arrived, I met her cook and her children and I said, "Come on outside; we'll sit on the grass at the back of the house and I'll throw the bones just for you and the servants at this time." So I started to throw, and she said, "Well, we'd like to show you the problem." I said, "Show me what?" And she walked away and came back with a totem doll, burnt black, and a crucifix burnt black. All the clothing was gone — it had been burnt — and all the hair was gone; all that was left was the wood. I said, "Where did you find that?" and she said, "buried underneath the back steps, so that every time we walked in and out of the house we were walking over the evil of this totem." I told her, "South African tribes don't have such totems; there is no such thing," but she said, "That's where we found it. Our little dog dug it up." I thought that very strange. A totem and a crucifix. And this was a Jewish family.

I threw the bones and completely diagnosed the servant. No

problems there. She was very worried about the household, the children and all. She and the madam were very close. I asked her to take the little ones away, as I wanted to be very frank with the mother, so off she went to play with the children in the front garden. Whilst this was going on the husband came home from work, which is what I had hoped would happen. I had already started finding that the problem in this house was the husband. I told him to take off his shoes and come sit down with us. This was a powerful, aggressive, difficult, awful man. I could see that the wife spent her whole life with the maid, crying together, and that she dreaded him coming home. But what did it have to do with the totem? Where did it all fit in?

I finished reading the bones on the wife, talking about how good she was and mentioning all her strengths, so the husband could hear. He then asked if he could speak, and I said yes, but first I wanted to know what he could tell me about the totem and why it was so burnt. He replied in a very short, cold, businesslike manner: "Our dog dug it up, and I could see that it was a totem that would put evil on us, and we'd been walking in over it. . . ." He had obviously read a few books he'd obtained from the library and he was going to let me know that he knew all about this stuff.

He didn't know that totems are not found among South African tribes. He said, "I brought it out here and I made a fire and said to my wife, 'we're going to burn this and get rid of it' but it wouldn't burn. And that's when I began to get apprehensive. It's wood, but it's only charred; it wouldn't burn away, even though it was in a big fire. So I said to my wife, 'Right; we'll use a crucifix.'" "But you're Jewish," I said. "Yes, but I know the power of the cross. So I made a crucifix and I tied it on and that wouldn't burn either." "Understandably so," I said. "Sir, I now understand that you are dealing with something you do not understand at all. It is a very powerful influence, a totem, but I'm a bit non-plussed at the moment because we don't have any in our South African tribes. But thank you for that story, and now will you just sit there."

I thought about this for a while and then said, "There's a black man, here, from far to the south." "Yes," he said, "I have a man from Zululand." Well, that was it. The Zulus know a great deal. They are very advanced as a tribe. This man would have heard of totems, to the north, and would just have carved one, a simple thing to do, and he would have buried it there, hoping that they would find it, because the relationship in this house with this man and his staff was absolutely awful, and obviously this Zulu didn't like him. He was going to leave, but he wanted to leave a bit of influence there.

The common thing to do is to urinate in a gourd or a melon set in a ring of stones. That sort of sign on a property lets the occupants know it's being "fixed." I don't know how much power they actually have, but it certainly has an incredible psychological power over people who believe in it. Whites know about this; it's common knowledge. They will phone me up and say "There's a spirit that's affecting my servants." The servants won't sleep there, because the spirit comes at night. That's why they all put their beds up on big paint tins, so the spirit can't climb up and get into bed with them and fix them. Whites know about these spirits, but they don't know what to do about them, so they phone me up and say, "Could you come and take the spirits off my property?" When they see unusual things they will accept that it's a black influence, evil, on the property.

So this Zulu, I am convinced, carved that totem, having heard about them, and thought, "That'll fix them," and dug it in shallow and loosened the soil, because he wanted that dog to dig and dig it up and he wanted that man to find it. He wanted to destroy this man, but not physically. I was convinced that was what it was.

I said to them, "You're quite right: The evil is attached to the totem, and I'm taking it home with me. He asked me, "Are you not concerned about taking the evil home and putting it on your property?" I told him, "Oh, no, no, no, I've had plenty of experience with this. I'm far too powerful." In fact, I've still got the thing, somewhere! I said, "It cannot possibly touch me," and he fully accepted that my power was so strong that there was no spirit that could touch me or frighten me. So, I was finally able to home in on him, and I gave him the dressing-down of a lifetime, because I was the only one who could tell him straight to his face how horribly he was behaving. And he finally woke up to the fact that he had a lovely wife and beautiful children and a wonderful life. He actually admitted his faults. And I told him, "I'm going to do you the greatest service. I'm going to take away evil that was placed on you, and I'm doing it for nothing. I'm going to take that doll home and clean it, and I'm going to cleanse your property. I'm going to leave you with a perfect situation, so make damn sure you live with it right." And he did. Not that a miracle happened; the man didn't overnight become a saint. But he certainly changed for the better, and they all were much happier.

When I told Phineas about it, I asked him if it were possible that that totem could actually have affected them, and he said, "Well, we don't really know," but it was the Zulu's way of setting things straight. He placed that doll there because he thought, "Someone has to bring this out in the open and let this man know that what he's doing is unacceptable." And what a wonderful way to do it, because then I was sent for! You have to destroy the man, undermine him, and then build him up and set him on a different path. And that's exactly what happened. Isn't that incredible?

How do you cleanse a property? You have certain herbs and you put them in a container with water (very dramatically, of course!) and you use your stick. You mix up the herb, froth it up a little bit, then walk round the property and cleanse it.

We were called once by a young man, a friend of my children in his early thirties. He had a factory. He was very progressive, in those days, when most people weren't: He had Coloured, Indian, and black staff, and he treated them as complete equals. And they took advantage of him. He didn't know what to do, because he couldn't change his ways, but the factory was a complete failure. He loved everybody and wanted to help them all, but you see, blacks don't like weakness, and that's how they saw him. They like fairness, but they like strength. They want to hear No and Yes with equal firmness, which this youngster didn't do. He came to me in anguish, asking for help. I told him, "All right, don't worry. I'll fix it."

I got Phineas and said to him, "Now we're going down there, and they're not going to give us anything, but we must help this young man." You see, Phineas always got paid; this was his job. But I never even wanted a bar of chocolate, because I mustn't.

We arrive at the factory, Phineas just gets out of the car, and I pick up all the stuff. He's wearing a suit and tie; I'm wearing tribal garb, walking behind him and carrying his briefcase and my own bag! When I'm in Venda, I don't carry anything, but when I'm with Phineas, he's the Senior.

The stage is all set. The blacks see our necklaces, they know what they mean, but they are agog at a white and a black *nyanga*, in their factory. I call for someone to sweep the floor in the middle of the factory, and I spread a skin and a mat and I take Phineas' briefcase and we take off our shoes. I undo the briefcase very ceremoniously and take out meercats and mongoose whole — they've been skinned whole, emptied out, cleaned and stitched up, and they are now containers. There are plenty of medicines of all kinds. I place them all carefully beside the mat, then take out the gourds and anything I think he might need to use, and his skin bag with the bones. I take out his stick and hand it to him, and he sits down on the floor and just waits. Then I unroll my mat and take out my bones, and I say, "We will not throw for one person here. My master says we will throw for the whole factory." So nobody will breathe into the bag. You see, if one person breathed into the bag, the reading would be just for him, and we had to treat them all at once. Nobody questions it or asks, "Why are you here?" or "What's wrong with the business?" because they know.

I bang my bag on the ground and I throw — Phineas is the Master, so he just sits there. I do a superficial reading, about positives and negatives, and I say, "There's a very big problem, here. We can feel a great disharmony and now we will identify the people related to that disharmony." Now those who have actually stolen from the owner are sweating. It's not difficult to see which ones they are. And then I turn to Phineas very dramatically and ask if he would like to take over, and he comes forward and he throws, and of course he can pick them out. He's been at this all his life! "I wish to speak to YOU, and I wish to speak to YOU, and YOU will please come down here," he says to several of the people assembled. (All the factory workers, black, white, Coloured and Indian, are there, watching and listening.) By this time, I must tell you, they all are quite frightened.

We tell them all that they have been possessed. We don't want them to lose their jobs, after all, just to stop stealing from the owner. We tell them they have been overcome by evil spirits and that we are going to cleanse them, that we are going to get it right, so that no more will there be any problems in this factory. And then we do a cleansing. I hold the bucket and Phineas walks round the factory, cleansing it. Now you must realise that, in that political period, to see a white woman carrying a bucket for a black man, that alone was significant, and to walk one step behind him had incredible significance! We knew what we were doing, and the power of it, and the proof is that the young man didn't have any more stealing in his factory.

We've cleansed restaurants, even churches. Phineas and I together. That's why we're so close. We've rendered service in so many places. Once an Afrikaner woman called me in a terrible state. There was a problem with her little child, and it was urgent. They lived in a town some miles away. Off we went, and when we arrived the woman drew me aside and whispered that she feared blacks. I assured her there was nothing to fear in Phineas, but I told him to sit on the opposite side of me. She didn't dislike him, but she was terrified of him. We all took off our shoes and sat on the floor and started to throw, and it was extraordinary. We discovered that this child lived with nightmares. It just didn't sleep. That was there so strongly. Dreams send messages. The blacks tell you your brain is the same at night as during the day, so why do you think it is not telling you something when you dream? You must not discard this information; you must use it, as you do when you are awake. The messages that come to you often have a very strong reason. That's why, when Phineas has a problem he cannot solve, he will take a piece of your hair and put it on his pillow and sleep with it, hoping that when he is calm and at peace the brain will interpret it better at night, and then he'll have a dream and in the morning will work with that.

So why should this young child, night after night, have a nightmare and wake up screaming in the middle of the night? I said to the mother, "It has something to do with the grandfather, with your father," and she said, "That's right. Would you like to know my father's name?" I said, "Yes" and saw there was no connection at all among the family names. Why did she ask if I wanted to know the name, I wondered, and I threw the bones on her father. I saw right away and told her, "There's a very deep unhappiness from your father to this child and it's disturbing the child in his dreams." She said, "Yes; my father wanted us to call the child by his same name and we didn't."

You see, that is the force. I can't pick up a name, of course, but I could pick up that the grandfather was desperately unhappy about this child. Afrikaners usually call their children after the grandfathers — it's common. And he was deeply disturbed that his grandson didn't have his name. So I said, "Let's see how serious it is." Phineas immediately related to the continuity of a name and the power of it, because that's very black, as well. And so he threw and threw again and then said to the woman, "Why destroy your child for the sake of a name? Why don't you have the child renamed and call him after the grandfather? I'll see if that would make it all come right." And he threw again and said "Yes, all you have to do is change this baby's name," and they did, and the child never had another nightmare. It was the grandfather's spirit, continually going through the ether at this child, and she said there used to be knockings on the roof, as well. I'm sure the grandfather didn't mean evil to the child at all; it was in his subconscious, a bitter disappointment.

It was always for unhappiness in human behaviour that we were sent for. The work with blacks is almost always emotional; with whites I would say it is ninety percent psychological. If they have a physical problem they go to their own doctors, but they come to us if they have a problem destroying them in their minds. Blacks often come for physical ailments as well, which we treat with herbs. There are many wonderful medicinal herbs out there which are quite effective. The difficulty the white doctors have with this profession is that, with many of the serious diseases, the blacks wait too long to seek treatment and then it's too late.

The herbs are used by *nyangas, mungomas,* and *sangomas.* Phineas doesn't go out and dig them up himself; he sent me to Ndora Thivhusiwi to learn what to pick. She's very good at collecting herbs so the people in town are prepared to pay her to collect for them. It's hard work. You go out early in the morning, taking an adze and digging sticks and cutting tools, and collect the leaves — that's easy — and certain branches with bark, that's easy. The roots are not easy. There's one particular root called *mobadale,* found only in a thicket, which is very difficult to get. We would go out in a group and they would say to me, "since you're the new one, you must dig this root." And, getting all scratched up, I would get in there and dig and dig with the adze, and Ndora would shout out, "Leave some behind." Just like the Bushmen: You don't take it all; you leave some for the future. Everyone who is close to Nature knows exactly what to do. Once you have the *mobadale*, if someone offered you Ten Rand for it, you wouldn't sell it, because you know what it has taken to get it — it's a lot of hard work!

You take home this root and peel off the bark, working over a bowl or a mat, because you're not going to get a lot from it and immediately underneath the bark there is a thin red layer, very narrow, all round, and when you scrape off just the red, from that big piece of root, you'll have a half-teaspoonful. That's your multi-vitamin — a wonderful multi-vitamin. It's a most incredible tonic, one that is used for women who bleed after childbirth. It's expensive, because it doesn't grow below the tropics and other tribes don't get it very often. But they know about it and about how powerful it is.

Then we would collect berries and an assortment of other things many people know about. One root you boil, and from this one it's just the water you use. Another we would roast in the fire and pound it. There's a multitude of things out there. The *Voortrekkers* knew all about them — they used a great deal of them. People have forgotten, but not fully. There are still people who do not do this professionally but who use the natural herbs a great deal. It's not just herbs, it's all kinds of roots and vegetables, and all of them out there who are in this profession automatically know where to go, because they know what's in the dry areas and what's in the wet areas. It's a concept of Nature that's a part of your being. You don't have to study it. It's passed on by word of mouth, and all these women who were out walking learnt as we went along. But it wasn't only that. It was the bond of friendship that grew up between us, and we did so many things together.

I have gone out and watched the gathering and have learnt a great deal about the plants, but I have not become involved in producing medicines because that was not my interest. If it were, I could have set myself up as a herbalist. But I was interested in the psychological aspects of witchdoctoring. I had to have a knowledge of what Ndora was doing but it was not necessary to do it in depth. There seems to be a simple, straight-forward herbal remedy, out there, for most things.

One day Ndora sent a message through someone that she was coming to town to stay with me. Now, what to do with a witchdoctor in this environment? I said, "Fine," — no doubt about it — but I knew I couldn't have her staying with my servants, who might not like to have an *nyanga* out there with them, so obviously she had to stay up here. She doesn't speak a word of English. I said to my cook, each morning, "Ask Ndora what she wants to do today. And how long has she come for? How many days?" Because, you see, I had to drop everything; she was helpless here. She was in my environment, now. She never leaves me alone, when I visit her, so I can't just say, "Sorry, I'm off to Council now." I must care for her whilst she is here. But she knows that I am under great stresses of other work. So it was three days. "She wishes to go to town to go shopping with you," my cook told me. Ndora also told her what she wanted as a gift from me. The custom is that you always give a present, no matter how humble. I often give porcupine quills. They are the greatest tool for opening up sores, exactly like injection needles. If you want to get medicine in, you use a porcupine quill. Porcupines aren't so prevalent, anymore. You rarely see them as we did twenty years ago. I always keep a great pot of porcupine quills and wrap some up to take with me wherever I go. It's a great present. Presents don't have to be money.

Ndora told my cook she wanted some flour and some soft velveteen slippers. So I took her down to where the Indians have their *muti* shops, and did we have a day! I think we laughed from morning 'til night. Before we left here, I said to the cook,

"We're going to be out all day, and we're going to have to eat, so ask her if there's anything she wants to say to me now." We don't meet many Vendas in town. There are people from many other tribes, but not the Venda. Now there are more than there used to be, but in those early days you had to look for them. I knew I wasn't going to find anyone in the street who could speak Venda, and she didn't speak any other language. So we set it all up, I thought quite well, and off we set, the two of us, laughing and having a great time. She carried a bright red handbag, which I had given her, and her muddy clay hair was all covered up with a nice doek [bandanna], and there the two of us went off in my car, as any two old friends.

We go to the first shop, where they have every pair of slippers it is possible to have, all out around her. But it's No to every one. The shop people wanted to know who we were, and I explained that we were two *nyangas*, that Ndora was from Venda. There was no way she was going to buy those slippers in Shop One. She didn't buy them in Shop Two, Three, Four, Five, Six, Seven, Eight, Nine, or Ten. She was having a ball! And by this time, everyone knew that she wasn't going to buy them yet. Why hurry? Then she bought a pair almost exactly like the first ones she saw, but it didn't matter, because by that time she had established in the whole of that area, that territory, who we were! And we were having all sorts of people popping in and out and greeting us. By this time I had overcome my "white" concept of, "You know, we really ought to buy something now." We went from shop to shop, and then we went to the *muti* shops. Again she didn't buy — she could get more than they can — but we went in and greeted everybody and she inspected everything, and she didn't know that she couldn't go behind counters, so she did, and they fell in love with her, and we had a wonderful time and we laughed and laughed.

Lunchtime. I could have got take-aways and sat in the park, but that wouldn't have been a challenge of any kind. So I went to the Carlton Hotel, which is the biggest, most expensive and exclusive hotel in town and which hadn't been there very long. It was VERY exclusive, but I knew we wouldn't get thrown out. It was multi-racial because of the overseas blacks from America. It was the one place I knew we wouldn't get thrown out of. Otherwise, it was take-aways in the park; there were no other restaurants where I could go with her. So, we went to the Carlton Hotel.

Now, I didn't have on special clothes. I wasn't going to look like a white boutique lady whilst I was out with her. I had on very ordinary clothes and of course my African beads. We walk in the front door of the Carlton Hotel together, and she doesn't know this is strange, so she's completely relaxed, and so am I.

We get to the restaurant (it's so *posh* I'd never even been there with Cecil, at that time) and out comes a man, whom I greeted in Zulu, as I could see he was a Zulu, and I said to him, "I don't know whether you have Venda waiters; we two speak very little English, but we speak very loud! He went into the kitchen and found us a Venda who came to our table, and I explained, "Now we'd like you to do a little interpretation here. You have here, for a very super lunch, please, two *nyangas* from Venda." And the Venda starts talking flat-out to Ndora! To her it doesn't seem like a miracle. Of course I would find someone for her, make her comfortable, as she did for me! The young man asked, "Who are you?" "What do you mean?" I replied. "You can SEE who we are." "BOTH?"

"BOTH! She works with me!" Well, they accepted it. The Zulu now knows he's got to take care of us; the Venda goes back to the kitchen, and we're brought the biggest steaks in the Carlton Hotel. And I said, "I know the way she makes *putu* porridge. I don't suppose you do that here, but do the best you can. You don't have any caterpillars, do you?" "No, Madam," he replied seriously! But we had a meal with which Ndora was more than a little bit comfortable.

Everyone in the restaurant was watching, and you could see they were all curious because this was the only table that had so much black staff hovering round it. You could see they were all wondering who we were. They figured she must be a black royal or something, and that I was looking after this princess. I don't know what they thought, but they were fascinated. It was all they could do to keep their fingers off their cameras! It was so funny, because they were all tourists, and they were calling their own waiters over and asking, "Who are those two over there?" And they said, "Oh, they are very special people in our black society." So that was our lunch. It was a day I'll never forget. It cost me a lot of money, but it was worth it! For Ndora, it was no more than expected. When I visit her she lays it on for me. And if I need someone to speak English, she'll find someone who's had a bit of English — a schoolteacher or something. So obviously I would do the same for her.

It was all so ordinary, and yet it was so special. When I came home and told Cecil, he couldn't believe it. He couldn't believe I would go that far. "And nobody threw you out?" he asked. I said, "They dared not. I let them see exactly who we were." We agreed that it was great.

Ndora often would take me to her ceremonies. She didn't have the same set-up as Nellie — only three acolytes. But as she was a great herbalist, she regularly had patients there for treatment — often very dramatic, with the killing of a cock and a goat and all. One day she sent for me because a lady had arrived from Cape Town, and that was quite special. So I set off and when I get there I go down to the *kraal* and there's this Xhosa woman, from the Cape. Now that's over a thousand miles from there. She'd come by train, over two nights, then out by bus. She was beautifully dressed — Western clothes, handbag, shoes, the lot. And she spoke perfect English. I greeted her in Venda, but she said, "I'm afraid I don't speak Venda." "OH!" I replied. "Good afternoon, Madam. What is your name?" She loved being called Madam. "My name is Elizabeth." She didn't tell me her Xhosa name. And I asked, "Why are you here?" "I have extremely bad bronchitis. My lungs are full of pus and liquid, and I've come for treatment." I said, "A thousand miles you've come?" "Well," she said, "it's very well known that the Shangaan and the Venda are the very best teachers, at the moment." (As I've told you, it's remained that way.) I asked her what she did for a living and learnt she was a Nursing Sister in a hospital in the Cape. I said, "You're WHAT?" and she replied, "I'm a Sister-Tutor." "And you're sitting HERE? You know, Elizabeth, I'm a Nurse, from a hospital. I was a Sister, never a Sister-Tutor, but why are you here?" "I'll tell you afterwards." I asked what they were charging her and learnt it was £10 [$40]. Now that was a lot of money, then. And she'd had to pay all her railway fare, to and fro.

That day we started doing the preparations. The acolytes washed blankets and we were given rattles for our legs, and Ndora and I went out for herbs and she dug up certain roots and things and we brought back a whole basket full of stuff. The next day I was down there early in the morning. They had built a big fire and on the fire was a big iron pot of water boiling. Around it, in the fire, were some very big stones. Round stones. There are plenty of round stones, there, in the river. Over that, the men Ndora had called in were putting up a shelter. They put up forked sticks and roped them together, with cross beams, and over that they put a lot more sticks and then made a blanket house. All over the fire. In the meantime, Elizabeth, in the house, had taken off all her clothes — this Westernised Sister-Tutor — and was wrapped in two blankets. She joined us outside.

We, by this time, were in full regalia and singing and dancing and the drums were going. I had asked Ndora what exactly we were going to do, there, but she just grinned. Eventually, when the moment was really humming — and I must tell you, you get high very easily with all that excitement — then Elizabeth was put inside the "house," the blankets were taken off, she sat in there stark naked, and into the boiling water they threw all the herbs we had collected, and the big stones. There you have an instant inhalation. The more she coughed, the more herbs they threw in, then some more big stones and it went on for quite some time — five to ten minutes. I said, "Wait a minute. Third-degree burns. It's HOT in there, you know. I don't think she can handle this. Let's get her out." They looked at me as if to say, "Not to worry" and put more herbs into the pot. She was coughing so that I thought she was going to bring her lungs up.

Eventually she came out, wrapped now tightly in blankets. She was sweating from head to foot, dripping with sweat. Into the huts, water prepared — the tin baths were there — and into the bath. We bathed her and cleaned her and put back on her Western clothes, all calmly and relaxed. Then we sat down at the table and tea arrived! It was marvelous. The tray of tea, the jar of condensed milk. And we all had tea and something to eat.

We'd killed a cock and had put the feathers into the inhalation as well. Symbolism, of course: The leg feathers go into the pot to tie the spirit of the cock to the medicine that's curing the patient. Later that evening we cooked the liver and cooked the chicken and ate it. Those are always for the witchdoctor, along with the goat. But the symbolism's always got to be tied to it.

"Now, Elizabeth," I said, I'm so glad your English is good. Tell me exactly what has happened here." "Well," she replied, "if I had told the doctors at home, in my hospital, they would have put me onto hourly inhalations, and it would take me about a week, wouldn't it?" There it was. Her lungs were completely clear and her temperature was gone. Instant, you see. Because those herbs were pouring into her lungs. But I think it's only because of generations of the strong surviving and the weak babies dying that she could take it. You see, those herbs went right down into her lungs, and the more she coughed the deeper they went. And she was completely cured. She told me, "That's the best Ten Pounds I've ever spent." A Westernised black — quite high up the ladder in Western medicine — went back to basics when the need came. It was fascinating. And the very fact that we sat there chatting in English, over tea, was incredible. I asked if, when she went back, she was going to tell the doctors what she'd done. "No," she replied sadly. The Western doctors, where she worked, would think she'd just gone home on holiday to visit her mother. Many of my friends can't understand this, but to me it seems quite reasonable. You see, blacks have always reared the strong. Whites have always reared the weak along with the strong. So there are certain things blacks can do, or survive, that we cannot — because we're not physically able.

Ndora was not married. She never felt the need for a husband. Her life was complete without one. She was always surrounded by her acolytes and was busy with the various ceremonies and training.

I'd like to tell you a tale of what happened to Nellie, the *sangoma,* when she was taken ill. She was taken to the nearest missionary hospital. She tried herbs on herself, as she would have on a normal, everyday basis. But this time she was very ill. She was about fifty years old at this time. The missionaries asked if there were anyone she would like to phone and she asked to phone me. Her message was straight forward: You must come; I need you. She wanted me at her bedside; she wanted me to hold her hand. She was a very strong, powerful *sangoma,* but she wanted me with her. Everybody, at some stage, needs some help. And that is what this business is all about: Never ignore a plea for help, no matter who it comes from — a man sitting under a tree or a high government official. I have had managing directors of very large companies come up to me at a meeting and whisper in my ear, "I need your help." It's the bones they want. It's not Rae Graham. It's anonymous and it's private. A managing director cannot confide in his committees, because he's the first person they will whisper about in the corridors.

The wife of the head of one of our largest companies came to me for help. To the outside world she may have seemed to have everything, but what she didn't have was someone in whom she could confide. This is the function we serve — for people at all levels.

ADVENTURES WITH PHINEAS

I once went to a meeting with Phineas with a large group of very influential people in town. This group had a lot of non-white workers — blacks, Indians, and Coloureds — and wanted to get to know them better and asked, as I was known as "The Bridge," would I come and give a lecture to a large group of them in a hall in town. Now this was a heavy responsibility for me, as I'm selling a principle and a concept, so I decided to take my teacher, Phineas, with me, which I did on some occasions — not just to do "the work," as he says. We weren't doing "the work"; we were selling South Africa. He goes with me, knowing full well he won't get paid, but he believes in what we're doing. He loves South Africa with a passion as deep as mine. So off we go. He asked me, "How important is this?" and I said, "Very. A lot of influential people in commerce and industry." "Oh," he said, "let's go and pick up the *mungoma*, Michael Moeketsi Moeng." So off we go to Randburg to pick him up and the three of us go to this meeting, and when we arrived even I got nerves, because it was a very large group of people and you get the feel of an audience. It was a very important meeting. My two friends said, "We're not going to demonstrate in front of that lot," and I said, "OK, leave it to me. I'll do all the talking. You just be there and give me all the support I need, the vibe." And they sat, one on each side of me on the stage, and I started my talk.

I described a black homeland, which most of them had never been to, not then. People didn't go to them then. It was too remote, the roads were bad, it was 350 miles to the north: "At Louis Trichardt take a right, then out to the Limpopo." People didn't go there. They had no reason to go there. This was around 1980. I described the black world, the black life, then alternative patterns of medicine. The people in that hall had said they wanted to understand their employees better. So I took out my bag of bones and I threw it on the floor.

Whilst I was discussing how a reading was done, I felt a very powerful force coming from one woman. You can't do a reading for a whole room, as there are too many vibes coming from different people, but this force was very strong, from a woman right in the middle of the audience. I looked straight at her and asked, "Madam, you wish me to help you?" "Please!" she replied. This happens often, in audiences. There is someone who is desperate to be cared for and helped, and you get their vibes. It's not difficult to pick that up. And so I called her forward and she took off her shoes and sat on the floor, and you can imagine that that, alone, was an unusual thing for anybody to do at the time, in front of whites. And they all got up on their chairs, and the whole hall was excited, and there was a tense feeling in the atmosphere — looking and watching and silent. I started to read for this lady, in the normal way, from the beginning, describing her home and her back-ground and her family, and everything was fine. I got to the health bit and was about to continue when Phineas leant over my bones, not his. I read my own bones very well, but I don't read Phineas' well. You get very closely affiliated with your own bag, what you have collected. Every piece in there has come from you; you found it. And although maybe the symbols are the same, the bones are not quite identical to someone else's. Just as I remember, as a nurse, that doctors would say that certain instruments — this is a black phrase — felt "kinder" in their hands than others (Africans will always say, "Make a tool that is kind in your hand," a beautiful phrase), my bones are very much mine. Here Phineas was, reading my bones, not well but not badly, when suddenly the *mungoma* leant over and pushed both of us aside. He was seated on a chair high behind us. I was on the floor, and now Phineas was on the floor, and Michael just leant over us and said, not reading my bones, just talking, and not in a trance, but not relaxed and ordinary either — he was in a special sort of spiritual state — he said to this woman, "I can see inside your head, and your skull is broken in many pieces. But it is now healed. It is no problem for you. Your head, you need not worry.

Accident, but no problem." (Later, we checked and learnt that the woman had been in an accident and had had a fractured skull.) Then he said, "But what you worry about is here," and he pointed to her breast. "It is gone and you are worried about the little lumps." That would be the lymphatic glands. And she was. She'd had a breast removed for cancer, she'd had all the X-ray treatment, but she was worried sick, even years later — she'd had this done some time ago — she was still worried sick and probably dreamt and slept with this thought: Will it come back in the lymphatic system and will I get more cancer? He told her, "You need not worry about the little lumps; they are clean and you are fine, Madam." And she looked at me with very wet eyes and said, "That was my worry."

Well, there was a tenseness in the room, and I could feel Phineas and Michael were now completely withdrawn and didn't want any chitchat. There was no way they were going to have a question time, which we regularly do in my lectures, and so I quickly turned to the chairman and said, "Please get us out fast. Not into the lifts, where other people are; just find us a way out. Get us into the kitchen or something." So he took us out through the kitchens and said, "Won't you have something to eat or drink?" I asked the two others, but they said, "We can't eat." I suggested, "Well, let's just have a cup of tea and relax." The blacks in the kitchen knew not to chitchat, as a white would have done. ("What happened there? What was that?") No, they just left us, very quietly. We stood in a clump in the corner and had some tea, then went down the fire escape to my car. We never saw or spoke to anybody else.

Whites may have thought that was very rude, but I could see and I could tell that my two dear friends were now remote from the situation and wanted to get away. We got in the car and drove north through Johannesburg and out to the suburbs. As we dropped off my teacher, he gave me a hug and whispered in my ear, "There's something not quite right here," and I said, "I know. I can feel it. I'll try and talk to Michael." Phineas said goodbye to me and off we went, because Michael lived many miles to the north and I had to drive him there.

After some time — there was a tense silence in the car — I said, "Michael, can I talk to you? Can I ask you a question? What happened there? I could feel it, and I apologise if I did something wrong." "Don't ever do that to me again," he said coldly. I said, "I knew there was something, but what have I done? What's happened?" "That woman needed me to help her," he replied. And I said, "You did a great job; it was wonderful, Michael, and she's gone home happy, now, and I sincerely thank you, on her behalf, and I thank you for showing the rest of that audience what a wonderful service is your profession, psychologically. Thank you very much." "But I am left inside of her. To do this you must have a proper ceremony. You do not do it like that." A lecture-demonstration was anathema to Michael. "I am inside her reading the cracked bones, which I saw. I am inside her looking through the cuts on the breast. I see that operation, I see those little lumps, I see everything. But I am now left still inside of her, because it was not done the right way. And now I shall have to go home for three days. I cannot work now." In other words, I'd taken away his practice; he couldn't perform anymore. "I will have to kill a goat and have a ceremony to bring myself back inside myself," he told me. His spiritual force was still in that woman, he firmly believed, and if he believed that, then that's the way it was. And so what I'd done, actually, was put him into a situation which was not acceptable to him.

By this time I'd been mentioned in the press quite regularly, often misquoted and often called a *sangoma*, which I am not and never will be. It's another leg of the profession which I do not do and never will do. I do not believe in the possession world and the smelling out and that whole format. For me, the beauty of the service of the *nyangas* and the *mungomas* is that it works. I'd like to mention, now, a part that doesn't work. In everything in life there's a good and a bad slice, and the slice I cannot accept I now speak of in my lectures to whites and blacks. I have now earned the right of complete equality with them, more or less, and can discuss the bad bits as well as the good bits. I can criticise, because I've earned the right for the No's as well as the Yes's.

The white doctors in the black hospitals saw the failures and that's why they lumped together all the witchdoctors, thinking they all were bad, and had no time for them. But now there's a large section of the white medical world that know all about it and accept some part of it. Certainly, there aren't a large number who accept all of it — I don't expect that. I only expect them to have an open mind and try to accept that perhaps some of it is good. There even are some who are learning to use parts of it.

What are the No's? The bad bits are the enemas. There is a belief that, if you're possessed below the waist anywhere, it is a spirit that's causing your other problem, whether it's a psychological problem or even an economic problem. So you've got to get rid of that possession. And they do it with enemas. There are various kinds. They take that yellow and black beetle, which eats your roses, and they bake those and make a powder and make an enema of them. They are highly acidic, they burn the lining of the intestine and cause septicaemia. It's the patient with the burnt-out intestine who gets admitted to hospital whom the white doctors see. They've got a septicaemia person who's going to die, and that's what they know as a witchdoctor's treatment. I fully admit that that is rotten.

But the psychological successes are many, and those the doctors never see. Let me give you one instance:

A black woman in Baragwanath Hospital had her breast removed for cancer, had all the X-ray treatment. All the nodes clean; fine. The doctors tell her, "Go home, Madam. You're fixed up," and she's discharged. Now that's when we get her as a patient, because psychologically she says to herself, "When I die, I will not go to live with my ancestors because I'm no longer a whole person. I'm only part of a person, so how can they have me up there?" And we have to do a long course of throwing the bones and building her up, telling her that she is complete, even without that breast, which was a dead, broken, cancer- ous old breast, and that in her spiritual world she is complete. In other words, that doctor's completely happy and has written on his file, "Successful — Discharged," but the patient now comes to another doctor. We have had other patients who have had complete medical treatment, but they're not convinced they're completely cured, and you know you can give yourself a bad headache with worry and can go on with manifestations of illness even when you're not ill. Like the little girl who couldn't walk.

We got into the lives of certain District Nurses, in Soweto, who would accept that their role could be a bridge like us. Now, when a woman comes to the hospital with twins, and one has a string round its neck with little *muti* bones and other little bits of medicines, the nurse knows instantly that they're going to an *nyanga*. She knows all the signs; she's black. And if she's wise, we try to teach her, she will say to the mother, "I have certain medicines that can cure this baby," and she convinces her to feed the child. Remember that, among blacks, when there are twins it is known that one is weak and one is strong so one must die, and they simply do not feed the weak one. That's like the Bushmen. They have to do that. There's no way a Bushwoman can survive with twins. I'm sure she's not happy about letting one die, but it's the law of Nature, just as in the animal kingdom. Fortunately, the blacks are beginning to learn.

Remember the missionary doctor friend of mine in Venda who convinced them to start rearing twins and the woman in her forties who, at a party one day, started singing and dancing with her sister in front of him and said, "Doctor, we love you. It's because of you we are both alive." He saw the results of his belief in rearing twins and then he used to preach and pray and say, "There is the result of my belief. You see, they are two useful human beings."

That was beautiful. He lived to see that. You don't always live to see the results of your input in life. So we would suggest to the District Nurses that they go to the *nyanga* with the mother and the twins and their *muti,* and take along the necessary antibiotics. There has been a great antipathy between those two professions. If you're black and have qualified as a Nurse, you tend to put tribal tradition behind you, because it is primitive and you've now advanced and you want to get rid of it. But now we're teaching them that there is good in all. You can still be proud of the past, but you re-use it. And she would say to this *nyanga,* "What exactly are you giving to these babies?" and, knowing that herb and knowing it was harmless, she would suggest to this woman, "We are so confident in what you are doing for that child, but may I also endorse it with my particular herb, which happens to be this white pill," and the mother then can be comfortable to use both. And that has begun to happen. Hallelujah!

In the Cape they suggested to the blacks who worked in the hospital that they plant a garden of herbs, so they could analyse them in the laboratories — a small miracle! Now, a white man and a black man in Durban have opened up a great nursery of the homeland herbs, which are planted and are being sold to the local *nyangas* and *mungomas*, instead of denuding the veldt. They are doing it in an organised fashion — a hundred of these and a hundred of those — and keeping the seeds so the plants are readily available, because sadly there are whole areas of the veldt where I go which are denuded of all the medicines. This was done not by the witchdoctors, who know better, but by those who have made a business of going out with great lorries [trucks] and collecting the plants to sell to the shops in town. At some of the private game reserves they have had their black staff go out and show them which plants they need, and they keep their own *nyanga* there to care for them and their guests. They asked me to come show them how to set it up.

I explained that they must build her a hut near a stream, as she must have access to her own water supply, and now she is there for the guests and can tell fortunes for them and make lots of money which she can put back where it is needed, in her village beyond the game reserve gates. The tourists have the fun of seeing a genuine herbalist and having a little bit of a reading, which is fun, and of seeing a herb garden and medicines in preparation. The *nyanga* has a full supply of the herbs she needs to take home with her for her own people and the veldt will not be denuded again. So that's another way of bridging, which is very joyful for me. All these outreach things are happening, and I've now been invited to many medical meetings and conferences where I can put on my costume once but then join them later at their cocktail parties and sell these concepts, mostly saying, "If you would study it more, you could accept the bits that work and discard what's wrong. Then the black will learn from you." That way, the blacks will be fully integrated into medicine in South Africa, which is what I want. It helps that, as a nurse, I can speak to these doctors in their own language and can show them the similarities between how I trained as a witchdoctor and how they trained in the wards. They relate to that.

Once I had a call from a Johannesburg hospital, from a doctor who told me they had gone as far as they could with a patient and needed tribal help, and that I was the only person they knew to call. I said I would only come with my teacher. I had only been at this for about five or six years at the time and didn't want the responsibility of making the diagnosis on my own. So I phoned Phineas to go with me, and I told him this was a very important case for us. We were being allowed our first visit inside a hospital. Never mind the lectures we've done, never mind the outside convincing of Sisters. Now we're INSIDE a hospital. "Do you realise, Phineas, this is such a breakthrough!" He arrived wearing a suit and tie and carrying his briefcase, as he always does, and I was as nervous as anything. But I believe so firmly in what Phineas has taught me. "Just relax, and the pattern will appear," I reminded myself. And it did.

We went into this ward and they were all fretting round — the doctors, the nurses, everyone. They asked what they should do and I told them to just stand against the wall. "And don't say anything." So they stood there, frozen like statues, not knowing what to expect, you see, and we go to the bed and see a black man who had been in a car accident and wouldn't move anything but his head. He believed he was completely paralysed. They knew he wasn't, in spite of having some broken bones. They assured me there was no way that man was completely paralysed. I had to know that medically he was able to recover.

Phineas never said a word. He was out of his element, in a hospital ward, where he had never been before. We stood on opposite sides of the bed and I took out my bag of bones and I just looked at the man and held his hands and put the bag of bones where he could see them and spoke to him in Venda. After greeting him and asking how he was, I explained that Phineas and I were both *nyangas* and that Phineas was my teacher. "We know that things are difficult for you here," I said, "in a hospital, with white people whom you may not be trusting. But we want you to know that we know that. We have come to help you in the way that you will understand."

I had him breathe into the bag of bones and tell me his name — he couldn't believe this! — and I threw the bones on the bed and started a reading. I only read it so far and then Phineas took over and read his bones and went in depth into the breaking of the body and how spiritually "the power" can bring it back, and that we were going to be that power so that he could walk again. He told him we would make him whole again, that there may be bits and pieces that are not quite as they were before, but that he would walk again. He didn't move, but he hung onto us with his eyes.

As a nurse I knew there would be a long period of therapy, much of which is based on desire, and I was explaining in my reading which was continuing even as Phineas did his — that the period for bringing the power back to his body would take time. And I told him that we could not be there all that time, but that we were going to bind him to that power, and I called for the therapist and put the patient's hands and the therapist's hands and Phineas's and mine all together and we held on to each other for quite some time. Phineas told the man, "We are now instructing these hands to do our work, because we have other sick people to go to," and the man accepted it and fully recovered and walked again.

What I can't say to you is how much got through to the doctors and nurses. I don't know. We may have affected them in such a way that future approaches to black patients will be slightly different. I certainly hope so. It's attitudes that I hammer at, time and time again. They are not yet ready to call us in regularly, as part of a team, but the relationship between black patients and their white doctors has been changed forever.

Interestingly, even as the blacks become more urbanised, there is an increasing need for *nyangas, mungomas,* and *sangomas.* They are needed to help ease the stress of the transition from Third to First World, Western life. I don't see that need going away, any more than the need for psychiatrists and their forms of treatment will disappear from Western society.

INITIATION
CEREMONY

O nce I got into the work and had done many trips out — I had done my cobra head and collected my bones — they were watching my acceptance of the program, I suppose, and it seemed to them OK to do my initiation ceremony. They asked Cecil to come along, as his presence would be important to me: I would need the psychological aid of the most important person in my life. The initiation ceremony comes sometime into your training — you could never handle this at the beginning — and the impact is that you are fully accepted everywhere. Up until then you are a Junior in training, so all my black friends were waiting for my goat ceremony. It is not the end of your training, just the end of your apprenticeship. In my case, the initiation came about a year and a half into my training.

I was surprised they asked Cecil, though I was delighted, and I was told I might also bring my children, but no visitors or friends. Just the immediate family. Only Clive and Natalie, of my children, were able to come.

I was asked to choose the date, one that would be propitious for me. I chose May 29, the birthday of my daughter Felicity, who was in America, so she would be with me in spirit.

We packed everything we could think of, for the trip. None of the blacks travelled from here with me; they were all already in Venda. We arrived in Venda, back at our old house, and Ndora immediately came to visit. She told me my ceremony would last two days, Saturday and Sunday. "On Friday," she said, "there is work you must do. Not the family; just you." "OK," I replied, "that's fine." On that day she came with a man to fetch me, and we went to buy my goat. That meant I had reached a very elevated position — a first for a white person. Though I knew nothing about the ceremony, I didn't ask any questions; I didn't want to know the answers at that point!

We went trotting off and had a wonderful time whilst I bought my goat. We had all the time in the world, so we didn't rush it. First you make friends with the people whose *kraal* it is. And I said, "I don't want to buy a very big one." There were goats bleating all round me and I thought, "One of you poor darlings is going to have to go." And they said, "That one's got twins," so I told them, "Let's take the weak one, as it's probably going to die anyway." So we did. It was a very formal transaction and and I had to pay cash, and everyone was all excited. They tied a rope on it and I walked home with this little goat trailing behind me. When the people in the village saw me, walking and trailing a goat, they all knew what was happening, though most of them had heard the news by then, anyway. I went to bed, waiting for them to come for me early in the morning.

That night there was a terrible storm, out of season. In South Africa, we know the seasons and what weather will come; you can count on it. We never have rain in May. But this night it was pouring with rain, and I woke up in the middle of the night and said to Cecil, "Oh, I'm all prepared for my new event and it's not going to happen. There's a storm out there and it's an outdoor function. It can't possibly happen."

In the morning, rather than the beautiful kaftan I'd brought to wear, I put on jeans and an anorak and rain hood, crying with the rain, and Ndora came running up and said, "What a blessing! The rain!" "Yes, I know you need rain," I said, "but what about my ceremony?" "Of course it's going to happen," she assured me. "This is more powerful than anything you could have done!" So I rushed to tell Cecil, and we loaded up the three-ton truck and the car with all the people. We were going to the *kraal* of Petros Nemaugani, the man who had decided that I was OK. This was very important and meaningful, as whoever's *kraal* was chosen would be strong for the rest of living memory. It will never happen again that they will have a white in this particular context.

So I was thrilled it was Petros. It couldn't be at the home of my immediate friends, Nellie or Ndora, and anyway it was exciting to have it someplace far away.

We loaded up the lorry [truck] with all the drummers, and all the women in their beautiful, best regalia, with all the beadwork, and I packed up my basket and off we went. The drummers in the back played for forty miles — in and out of rivers, up and down, over tracks and roads. It took ages to get there, and all the while it never stopped raining. The singing and the drumming were for me; it was a regular procession. I was in the first lorry, with Ndora and a man with whom I had worked a great deal; Cecil was behind, in a bakkie, with more drummers and some of the already-initiated witchdoctors of all branches; and behind him my son, in an automobile, with the local dignitaries.

The others in the truck with me had been very involved with me for a long time. There were many I had learnt to know, by this time, but these two were very close to me and they knew I would need people with whom I was strongly related to be my support team. They didn't choose people I knew superficially, which was kind. These two I was very strong with, and they started singing in Venda, and I joined in. Nothing binds you more closely than singing folk songs together. With the continuing rain and lightning and the three of us there together, I suddenly had visions of the witches in *Macbeth*!

We got to the foot of a little hill and of course the mud was terrible, so we parked all the vehicles and got out and walked, in the rain, in another procession. That's why black people walk in a single file: The more people who walk and pound the trail, the better the trail, especially for those at the back. They took out the drums, carrying them on their heads, and I was in front, sloshing through this black custard of mud. At the top of the hill was Petros, waiting for us with his wives, like a smiling Buddha.

When we arrived, Petros took me into a hut — a rectangular hut which is in addition to his half-circular and round huts. In the rectangular hut were a wooden table and some chairs and a paraffin stove and two lights. I unpacked my things and shook off the rain. As it was late in the morning, I suggested we make some tea. I wanted all my family to be completely relaxed, and I had brought a chocolate cake in a tin in a basket, through the rain, for the occasion. Petros understood this white behaviour and accepted it immediately. I had also brought proper cups and it was understood that they would be first for Petros and my husband and me, then for the men in the group, then Ndora, and then for as many others as we could provide for.

The tea was served and the cake was cut with the knife with which I eventually killed the goat. The drums had been taken into the big hut, where we were going to dance and where a fire had been burning all morning. They knew the drums would all be wet. They were placed round the fire and soon were taughtened up and back in tune. It wasn't long before the drumming started again and we could hear the music and the singing.

After a while they told me they must dress me and put me in my beads, so they put on my regalia and we went into the big hut, where I began to dance. All this time, my husband and children were right with me. Soon I was told it was time to leave, and we were led outside to where Petros kept his goats and they were sharpening my knife on a stone. He then gave the knife to me. "What have I got to do now?" I asked. "You've got to kill the goat, Mashudu, by yourself." Cecil looked at me and inquired, "Are you going to do that, Rae?" and I replied, "Yes, I am," whereupon he said to me, "Well, at this point, darling, I'm going round the other side of the hut!" And he did! My son and my daughter said they would stay. My son lasted a couple of minutes; Natalie never left me.

They had told me nothing of HOW I was to go about killing the goat. I asked, "How will I handle this? It's just a quick cut of the throat; I know that. But I can't hold the goat at the same time." So one of them held the two back legs and another held the front, whilst a third held its head for me, and I gave a quick cut across. Not knowing a goat's anatomy, I wasn't too sure of myself, but I knew generally what had to be done. It was over in a minute, and the moment it was done, feeling a great deal of relief, I shouted, "I did it! I did it!" Everyone was jubilant. Then I looked at them and said, "I'll bet I can skin a goat better than any of you" because the Bushmen had taught me and I knelt down and skinned it with great dispatch and to their utter fascination and delight. They had not known this about me. They called to everyone to come and watch me, and when I had finished, they made me show it to the crowd. I held it up like a matador. It was still raining; I was soaking wet.

Whilst I was parading round, the others had slit open the goat's belly and removed its intestines. Then they took the liver, which of course was given to Petros. He put it in a waiting pan on the paraffin stove and cooked it gently and slowly. That is the only part that may be cooked immediately; the rest of the animal was taken away and hung and I never saw it again. That was to feed Petros and his family — our gift to him. The skin was mine.

Then Petros said to me, "I need your bag of bones." He took out an *ndilo* bowl, the wooden Venda bowl used for many things. It's the dish in which you serve your husband the best food of the day; porridge is served in it, and pancakes. And it has its own very special carrying basket. It's like your Royal Worcester plates. Onto that he placed all my bones and he took the tail of a cow (his; I wasn't "there" yet) and placed it over the bones in the bowl and put it to one side. I hadn't known this, but early that morning Petros had gone out collecting fresh herbs — he doesn't ever use dried ones — to prepare a sort of stew. He poured this stew through the hair of the tail of the cow over my bones in the bowl. He then took the cooked liver and cut it up into pieces and brought it to me. "What do I do with that?" I asked. "First to your husband, the power behind you. Then to me. . . ." Of course I knew the pecking order, so I served Cecil and Petros and then my son. Then I took a piece for myself and then served the others, in order. It was necessary that I serve it; it was mine to serve. When I returned the basket to Petros, he took the *ndilo* and said to me, "You first, this time. We're making the bones strong for you. Drink through the hair some of the medicine, some of that water." I was a bit disconcerted because, while the liver had been quite clean, this could not be. The bones were not clean. Well, I said to myself, I've drunk other dirty things before, I suppose. So I knelt down and drank through the hair. The bones were removed and I served the bowl round to everyone else. Cecil was even more concerned than I, but he took a slight sip.

The rest of the day was quite easy. I went to the big dancing hut, where a line of people brought their sticks for me to bless. I danced holding each stick, to give it my power. This went on until dark. The drumming never stopped. In the middle of the night they called us into another hut. There, Petros had built a little "house" like I had seen in the bronchitis ceremony. I didn't understand, as I didn't have bronchitis. It was pitch black, except for a paraffin lamp, so it was full of "atmosphere." My family came in with me, but very few other people. Petros told me to kneel down by the fire. They brought in my bones, in the *ndilo,* with some herbs from the pot, and Petros said, "Now we are going to make you and your bones very strong. We are now binding you to the work." He directed me into the little "house" and they put a blanket over it, so I was inside the little sauna. Then he handed me some herbs — not wet, as the ones for the bronchitis ceremony had been, as an inhalant, but dry, to give off smoke, like incense. "Breathe it in," Petros told me. It was awful. Then he told me to drink some more of the medicine (broth) from the bones. I was being tied to my power in a symbolic way. Turning to Cecil, Petros said, "Put a coin in with the bones. You must buy in the ancestral spirit of Mashudu's great grandmother, so she will come to South Africa to watch over Mashudu." As Cecil did so, they mumbled something in Venda. Then they got up and marched round, chanting something which sounded very similar to Gregorian chant. Fascinating. The parallels to the Christian Church ceremonies, in all this, were surprising and incredible.

When that was over, I was allowed to wash and clean up a bit, as that was the end of the ceremony. After that, it was all fun. The drumming and singing and dancing went on all night. At the end we were physically and emotionally exhausted.

We went back to our Venda home — by this time it had finally stopped raining — and after a few hours' sleep, I went down to see Ndora and to see whether they were using my gifts. I had asked someone not connected with the ceremony what I should get for her, knowing she would be my main support during the initiation, and was told there were very set, specific gifts that one must give. It was mealie meal, sugar, tea, and other foods — but lots of it, to feed all the people. We had it delivered to her in the village. On the Sunday morning, I left my family to recover and visit friends on their own, and I made my way down to the village, where I learnt I had been expected. The celebrating had never stopped! They "knew" I would be pulled back there, that I would not just sit at home and have tea. Now it was the celebration part, the Thank You part. I've never had such fun. They gave me a drum and I played with the women, ate what they were eating (from the food I had sent), danced with them and listened to the songs they sang about me. This went on until about 4:00 PM. Then I was truly exhausted. Even those who had not been at the ceremony joined in the celebration day, and each of them came over to touch me and partake of my power. The whole village. It was quite an experience.

There was one disappointment, which I must recount. It was, perhaps, the only disappointment in my whole black life. At the end of the day, when I was packing up and looked round for my little goatskin, which obviously was very significant to me, it was gone. I was very upset. Everyone there was very upset and they all started looking round for it, but it was gone. Much later, when I came to terms with it, I realised that the person who had taken it must have had an incredibly strong need for my power, or to be associated with me. After all, that was a very special goat. I'm the only white who has done this ceremony, in Venda. So I understand. I'm almost sure it was a woman. I relate to her need, and I just hope it has fulfilled and given her the strength she required.

I had a similar disappointment with whites. When I was doing my early lectures, in Johannesburg, I spoke to an international society at a very significant club. I had put my notebook on the chairlady's desk, at the front where I was sitting, to use for reference during the question period after my presentation. At the end, of course, lots of people come up to speak to you, and at the end of that time I discovered my notebook had disappeared. Everyone looked, even for a whole week afterwards, but it never surfaced. I've thought about that a great deal. There were years of work in that notebook — notes, drawings, references. They would be useless to anyone else. Again it was a woman. (It had been a women's organisation.) And once again, it must have been someone who needed my power, who needed something of me. My notebook was the easiest thing to take. I just hope, whoever she is, that if she reads this book she will see this. I hope it produced some solution to her great need, because it was a very sad thing to do to me. And I still grieve it.

CASES

A white lady phoned to say she had problems in her outbuildings, her servants quarters. Her maid had left her — she didn't say whether happily or not — and from that day on, the white woman was unable to keep a servant for more than a week. Even girls who were without jobs and were desperate would disappear without asking for their money. Obviously the room had been "fixed" by the original maid who had left her. I reported all this to my teacher, Phineas, and he came and we did a full reading.

We discovered that a death, probably very violent, had occurred in that room, and so nobody could sleep peacefully. When the young women went to sleep there, the blankets were pulled off the beds whilst they were sleeping and the bed was rocked. Phineas put *muti* powders all round the room — our usual cleansing process — and he gave to the new servant woman some powders to put in her bath, to strengthen her, and we generally assured everyone that the restless spirit would now be quiet. The lady in question paid Phineas Ten Rand for this treatment, and a week later the report came back that all was well, the spirit was gone and the room was quiet.

What was interesting was my reaction to doing all these interviews, all over the area, with the white owners and their black staff. I would accept fully that Phineas could solve whatever problem came up. I never dreamt that he couldn't. Obviously, some relationships are very difficult and no one is one hundred percent successful at anything, so an occasional failure was acceptable. As we drove away, he would often say, "Well that was good; we helped those people." You must realise that Ten Rand is nothing [$4]; there are people in Soweto who charge R500 [$200]. A charge of R300 [$120] for cleansing a "fixed" place would be standard. There are people in Soweto who have cottoned on to this and who go round the rich white suburbs of Johannesburg knocking on doors, asking if there are problems among the black staff. Of course, there's hardly a house anywhere that doesn't have some sort of problem, and the people are quite willing to pay. And then they never see that person again. With Phineas, I am dealing with someone I know well. His whole family and mine are quite close and I believe and trust him completely. I would recommend him to anyone.

Another time we had a patient in Swaziland. He came in and complained of "a problem." That's all he told me. I began throwing and went through his body and I couldn't find an illness or any pain, but I found that he was sleeping very badly. He was getting a lot of bad dreams. He confirmed that that was so and told me he dreamt of three pairs of shoes. So then we threw again on that, but there were only two pairs of shoes. Now we knew what the problem was. Phineas took over and started to throw, and he said, "This is a story of the shoes being stolen. You dream of three but there are only two, and you wake up and think someone has stolen the other pair." He threw the bones again and found there definitely was a theft. "Ah," he said, "I see the thief, but he is not from here. He has come from very far and is not employed in the place where you work." Just by giving the man this information and reassuring him that it was no one near him, that no aggression was necessary, a bad situation was averted and no fights took place, because the man believed that the thief was very far away. He paid One Rand and left, very contented.

Generally speaking, people come to us for one of three problems: physical, emotional, or financial. Sometimes it takes a long time to reach a breakthrough, and we ask people to come back for other sessions. Especially when it is a question of building someone's confidence — as with a suicide case we once treated. Just like the Western psychiatrists.

We don't throw all the bones each time. On the first throw, we do, to get all the background information. Then, depending on what I find, I take the divining bones and those which relate to the particular problem. Different bones mean different things.

Once a young man came to the house and I had great trouble

reading him. I simply couldn't "see" anything. I folded up my mat and turned to Phineas and said, "I must be more tired than I thought, as I'm simply not getting anything," whereupon Phineas took out his bag and threw his bones. Again, nothing. Incredible. I turned to the young man and said, "I'm terribly sorry, but we just don't seem to be getting anything today. I'm afraid we cannot help you." He looked at me and asked, sheepishly, "Does it matter that I did not give you my real name?" Phineas could hardly believe what he was hearing. Of course that was why we got nothing. It turned out the man was a very well-known actor and didn't want to reveal his identity, and away he went.

I said to Phineas, "I don't understand this. Why should that be so?" He had no answer and told me only, "I do not question it." Just as the question remains unanswered as to how we read what we do from throwing the bones. It's a gift. Interestingly, most of the whites line up to see Phineas, whilst the blacks line up to see me. Everyone wants the power of the thing they don't understand or have. Even before I became a witchdoctor, when my children were growing up, I always "knew" which of their friends were in trouble and needed help. I could feel the vibes, just as I felt those of that woman in the crowded meeting hall. Now I no longer question it, either.

SEARCHING FOR AN EXPLANATION

I am often asked how all this witchdoctoring works, and of course in many instances there is no explanation, just as Phineas told me. But we know the mind is very powerful. I will never forget one well-known, highly respected white lady from the academic world. A highly evolved woman. She said to me, "Rae, I've come to you because I can't talk about this in my world, but I am possessed and there is something in my stomach, and until it's taken out I will never be a complete person again." I thought to myself, "YOU?" I know blacks talk like that but it was odd coming from her. I asked what she wanted me to do, and she said, "It has to be done a black way, doesn't it? I'm possessed. So it's got to be taken out the way our friends do it." I said, "Are you sure you want this? Because there's a ceremony you have to go through." "That's what I want, Rae."

I told her it couldn't be done in the city, that she would have to go to a village in one of the black homelands, and again she said, "That's what I want." I tried hard to explain to her that she was a Western woman and that it might be better if she went to her own doctor, but she interjected, "No way." She had been possessed in a black manner, she said, and only the black manner could take it out.

It was all up to her. She got on a train and went to the black homeland. She had to get the train to stop there, as there was no halt. The conductor on the train was very uncomfortable to let this elderly white lady climb down the side of the train into the veldt, not even at a railway siding. He was happy to let the blacks off because they lived there, but he knew she was going to a village where there were no other whites.

Off she trotted, through the veldt, with the people who had come to meet her, and she spent a whole weekend there, with the drumming and the mesmeric chanting and everything to put her in the right frame of mind. The nyangas came and danced round her and they operated on her stomach. No anaesthetic at all, but by this time she wouldn't have felt pain anyway, because she was so entranced with this wonderful thing she had finally got to happen. They cut her and she bled, of course, but they cleaned her up and produced a large dead lizard, which was taken out of her stomach. They gave it to her to keep and said, "There you are. That's what was giving you trouble. That's the spirit that had been laid upon you, and now you will be one hundred percent sure in your health and your life and everything else." And back she came on the train.

She came straight to see me and produced this lizard. She firmly believed that lizard had come out of her stomach. Now, you and I know it didn't, but she believed it. So from that day to this she's been fine! She was convinced that some black person had put a spell on her and that she'd been cured. Maybe she is right. I see her, now, at functions and out in society, and she gives me a smile and says, "I'm so well, Rae. I'm so fine."

How can I explain this to whites? I can't, so I don't talk about it, but I could give you many stories like that. How could I explain to them that if she firmly and strongly believes that some black has done that to her, there's no way any other cure is going to work. It's an attitude. I don't know what the answer is.

¥

MASHUDU'S "KIT"

(Ten years for completion)

<small>THE BAG OF BONES:</small>
Baboon, *two*
Springbok, *two*
Crocodile, *two from its tail*
Pig, *two*
Goat, *two*
Tortoise, *two*

Tiger cowrie shell, *one large*
Conch shell, *one*
Cowrie shell with a ring on its top, *one small*
Cowrie shell with spots on its top, *one small*

Almond shells, halved, *four*

Coins, different sizes and values, *four*
Wooden dice, carved, *four*
Ivory dice, *four*
River pebble, *one*
Fire symbol, *one*
Death symbol, *one*
Natural stones, symbolic for land, *two*

<small>ARTIFACTS:</small>
Wooden four-pronged stick, *one*
Fly whisk, from the tail of a cow, *one*
Tail of a wild animal, *one*
Hand-made knife, from natural elements, *one*
Beaded dancing stick, *one*
Stick with the tail of a horse, *one*

GLOSSARY

kraal	corral
mealies	corn
muti	medicine
spoor	tracks
veldt	grassy plain
Voortrekkers	Afrikaners who left the Cape for the interior
nyanga	herbalist, diagnostician
mungoma	specialist witchdoctor, psychic
sangoma	most spiritual of the witchdoctors, operates in a trance-like state